Contents

1 iPads for Productivity 7

2 Keyboards and the Apple Pencil 21

3 Productivity Apps 33

4 File Management 45

1 iPads for Productivity

The iPad has evolved into a genuine productivity option for the workplace, particularly with the release of the iPad Pro. This chapter looks at setting up an iPad so that it is ready for use in the office or classroom.

Why iPad for Work

When the iPad was first introduced in 2010, it was not considered to be a serious productivity device. It was aimed more at mobile communication and entertainment, in terms of using the web, email and text messaging and also music, videos and ebooks. There were some productivity options with the iWork suite of apps: Pages, Numbers and Keynote, which could be downloaded from the App Store, but the overall emphasis was for general consumer use rather than consistent use in the workplace.

As the iPad has evolved it has become more powerful, with the apps in the iWork suite becoming significant productivity tools, and a wide range of productivity apps for the iPad have been developed. However, the biggest step in the iPad becoming a genuine tool for the workplace was in September 2015, with the introduction of the iPad Pro. While it operated in most ways in the same fashion as the standard iPad Air and iPad Mini, it had a much larger screen (12.9 inches, measured diagonally, compared to 9.7 inches for the iPad Air and 7.9 inches for the iPad Mini) and, crucially, it supported an external Apple Smart Keyboard and also the Apple Pencil, which can be used for drawing on screen and also a range of navigational tasks. Although this does not replace the full functionality of a desktop computer mouse or laptop keypad, it has gone some way to enhancing navigation on the iPad.

In March 2016 a 9.7 inch iPad Pro was introduced, to give more flexibility to the range, for users who prefer a smaller screen for mobility. This has cemented the iPad Pro's position as a genuine option for the workplace or students: it has the power and functionality required for most productivity tasks and the range of apps, including productivity suites from Microsoft and Google, ensures that every angle is covered for the office or classroom. The iPad Air and iPad Mini can also be used for the same productivity tasks as the iPad Pro, but the Smart Keyboard and Apple Pencil make the iPad Pro the natural and most effective choice for the workplace.

Don't forget

The Apple Smart Keyboard and the Apple Pencil are sold separately from the iPad Pro. The Smart Keyboard also doubles as a cover for the iPad.

Don't forget

All of the iPad range (iPad Pro, iPad Air and iPad Mini) run on the same operating system (iOS) and have the same pre-installed apps.

iPads vs Laptops

One of the reasons for using an iPad Pro is to replace the laptop in the workplace or the classroom. While some people who have used laptops for decades may baulk at this thought, it is a realistic proposition that should be given serious consideration.

Pros

- **Size and weight**. Even the lightest laptops weigh more than the iPad Pro, which makes it a better option for taking between home and the office or classroom.

- **Range of apps**. The App Store has a Productivity category that contains apps for all but the most specialist tasks in the workplace. Also, a lot of these apps have sharing options so that content can be saved into different formats for viewing or editing on different devices, such as a Windows PC.

- **Connectivity**. Connecting to office networks is possible on the iPad Pro, through standard Wi-Fi settings, and there is also an option to connect to an office network via a VPN (Virtual Private Network) connection.

- **Smart Keyboard and Apple Pencil**. Used in conjunction with the iPad Pro, these devices provide the functionality that turn it into a powerful workplace tool.

- **iCloud**. Apple's online storage and backup service can be used to share documents with colleagues. For instance, you could create a document in Pages, save it to iCloud, and then share it with a colleague using Word on a Windows PC.

Cons

- **File structure**. The iPad does not have a conventional file manager so it can be more of a challenge keeping track of your files. However, the iCloud Drive provides a file structure for your online documents, and file manager apps can be downloaded from the App Store.

- **Compatibility**. Traditionally, file compatibility between Apple devices and Windows machines has been an issue. However, most productivity apps on the iPad can convert files into formats that can be opened by equivalent Windows apps.

- **Power**. Most laptops have more processing power and storage than the iPad Pro. However, much of this will be unused as most work tasks require less power than laptops possess.

If you use Microsoft Exchange in the workplace, an account for this can be added to your iPad via the **Settings** app. See page 173 for details about adding a new email account.

The Smart Keyboard and Apple Pencil cannot be used with the iPad Air or the iPad Mini. However, there are Bluetooth keyboards that can be used with them.

For more details about using iCloud and the iCloud Drive see Chapter Nine.

About the iPad Pro

Although the iPad Pro comes in two sizes, many of the specifications are the same for both. Also, the Smart Keyboard comes in both sizes, and the Apple Pencil has to be paired to the selected iPad version before it can be used.

Specifications

- **Storage**: Both models: 32GB, 128GB or 256GB.

- **Display**: 9.7-inch or 12.9-inch (measured diagonally).

- **Weight**: 9.7-inch, 437 grams (0.96 pounds) or 444 grams (0.98 pounds), for Wi-Fi/Wi-Fi and cellular respectively; 12.9-inch, 713 grams (1.57 pounds) or 723 grams (1.59 pounds), for Wi-Fi/Wi-Fi and cellular respectively.

- **Processor**: A9X chip with 64-bit architecture.

- **Cameras**: iSight camera (8-megapixels on the 12.9-inch model; 12-megapixels on the 9.7-inch model); FaceTime HD camera (1.2-megapixels on the 12.9-inch model; 5-megapixels on the 9.7-inch model).

- **Speakers**: Four audio speakers.

- **Microphones**: Dual microphones for video or voice calls and video and audio recording.

- **Touch ID**: This can be used to unlock the iPad Pro with a fingerprint. It is specified in the Settings app (see pages 16-17 for more details about setting up Touch ID).

- **Wi-Fi and Bluetooth**: Wi-Fi (802.11a/b/g/n/ac); Bluetooth 4.2.

- **Battery**: 12.9-inch model has a 38.5 watt-hour rechargeable lithium polymer battery; the 9.7-inch model has a 27.5 watt-hour rechargeable lithium polymer battery. Both models have a battery time of up to 10 hours for general use, such as surfing the web on Wi-Fi, creating documents in Pages, Numbers or Keynote, watching videos or listening to music.

- **Operating system**: iOS 9. All models can be updated at the same time when there is an update to the operating system. Check in **Settings > Software Update** for updates to the operating system.

Don't forget

The cameras on the 9.7 inch iPad Pro have a higher specification than the ones on the 12.9 inch model. The iSight camera is on the back of the iPad Pro and can be used for taking high resolution photos and videos. The front-facing FaceTime camera is best for video calling.

Don't forget

Both models of the iPad Pro have a Wi-Fi only and a Wi-Fi and cellular version. The cellular version can be used to connect to the internet, using a mobile/cellular provider. This is done through a nano-SIM card that can be used with this version of the iPad Pro.

iPad Accessories

As with most computer devices, there are a number of accessories that can be used with the iPad to increase its functionality:

- **Smart Keyboard**. This is available for use with the iPad Pro. It does not need any leads or cables to connect it to the iPad Pro; this is done with a Smart Connector. See pages 24-26 for details about the Smart Keyboard.

- **Apple Pencil**. Also available for use with the iPad Pro, this is a stylus that can be used to draw with great precision and perform some navigation functions. See pages 27-29 for details.

- **Covers**. All models of the iPad can be used with a Smart Cover. This provides protection for the iPad, acts as a stand for it and puts it to sleep when the cover is closed.

- **Stands**. There are a range of robust, folding stands that can be used to hold an iPad firmly in place in either landscape or portrait mode. They can also be used with a keyboard.

- **Adapters**. Longer Lightning to USB cables are available if the one that is supplied is not sufficient for connecting to a power source for charging. There are also adapters for connecting to an SD camera card.

- **Headphones**. If you are working on your iPad in an office environment and want to listen to music or video, a good pair of headphones is essential, so as not to disturb co-workers. Wireless and cabled headphones are available.

- **Speakers**. External, wireless speakers can be used with the iPad, for extra power and clarity.

- **Printers**. Wireless printers can be used with the iPad and there is a wide range available, from those for the individual to larger printers for business networks.

- **Wireless storage**. The iPad does not have a port for a USB flash drive, but there are wireless media drives that can be used to store and backup content from an iPad. They can be used to increase the storage on your iPad, and some also have a slot for an SD camera card for downloading photos. The drives come with their own app that is used on the iPad to access the wireless drive. One model to look at is the SanDisk Wireless Media Drive.

There are also a number of Bluetooth external keyboards that can be used with the range of iPad models.

The Apple Pencil can be charged via the Lightning Connector at the bottom edge of the iPad Pro. A full charge gives up to 12 hours of use.

Most accessories can be bought from an Apple retail store, or the online Apple Store (www. apple.com).

iPad Essentials

While much of the productivity on an iPad is done with specific apps for this purpose, there are still some basics that are important when using your iPad for work:

Don't forget

Tap on a setting in the left-hand panel to access its options in the right-hand panel. Tap this button **On** or **Off** for specific settings (green is On).

Hot tip

Folders (see next page) can also be dragged onto the Dock.

Don't forget

Apps can be removed from the Dock by reversing the process, e.g. press and hold on the app and drag it away from the Dock. This places it back on a Home screen.

1 Tap on the **Settings** app to access a wide range of settings. These can also be applied for productivity apps such as Pages, Numbers and Keynote. Swipe down the left-hand panel to view the Settings options

2 The options for settings includes apps that have been downloaded, such as the range of productivity apps

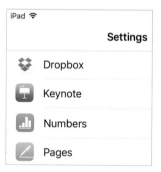

3 Press and hold apps to drag them onto the Dock. This makes them available on every Home screen

4 Press and hold on an app until it starts to jiggle. Tap on the cross to delete it

Built-in apps cannot be deleted from the iPad. These are the ones that are available when the iPad is first set up.

5 Drag one app over another to create a folder. Tap on the folder name and over-write it, if required

If an app is deleted it can be downloaded again, for free, from the App Store.

6 Double-press the Home button to access the App Switcher window. This displays all of the open apps. Swipe left and right to move between apps and tap on one to access it. Swipe an app up to the top of the screen to close it

Press and hold on the Home button to access the iPad digital voice assistant, Siri.

Swipe up from the bottom of the screen to access the Control Center with a range of quick actions. Specify its operation in **Settings > Control Center**.

Setting Up iCloud

When you first turn on your iPad there is a setup process covering a range of options such as language and location. Most of these can be specified, or changed, through the Settings app and do not all have to be selected during the setup process. One of these options is for setting up iCloud.

iCloud

This is Apple's online storage and backup service. You need to have an Apple ID to use iCloud and this can be created at the same time as you set up iCloud. To do this:

An Apple ID can also be created when you first set up your iPad. This is used for iCloud and also when you are using apps such as the iTunes Store, App Store, Messages and iBooks. If you do not have an Apple ID you will be prompted to create one the first time that you use one of the related apps.

The full range of settings options are covered in iPad in easy steps. Visit www.ineasysteps.com for more information.

For details about using iCloud with the iCloud Drive app, see page 167.

1 Tap on the **Settings** app

2 Tap on the **iCloud** tab

3 Tap on the **Create a new Apple ID** button and follow the wizard or (if you already have an Apple ID) enter your sign in details and tap on the **Sign In** button

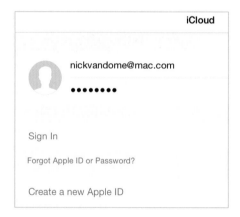

4 Drag the buttons to **On** to enable different types of content to be shared and backed up via iCloud

14

Accessing iCloud online

The Apple productivity apps, Pages, Numbers and Keynote can also be used with iCloud for storing documents. They can then be accessed with other Apple devices and also the online version of iCloud. This can be accessed at **www.icloud.com**

1 Enter your Apple ID details to access your iCloud account

When you create an Apple ID you will automatically create an email account that can be used via iCloud.

2 Tap on one of the apps to open it

From any app, tap on the **iCloud** button in the top left-hand corner of the screen to access the main iCloud menu, including an option for going back to **Home**.

3 Each of the apps contain any content that has been created within an iCloud-enabled app, e.g. Pages. If a document is created within the online iCloud, it will then be available through the compatible app on your iPad

From within an iCloud app such as Pages, tap on this button to create a new document (or click on the **Create Document** button).

Touch ID and Passcode

Security is a big issue in all areas of computing and this is particularly true in the workplace, where commercially sensitive documents may be held on computers. On the iPad Pro it is possible to protect your device with a six-digit passcode.
For greater security, the Home button can be used as a fingerprint sensor to unlock your iPad with the fingerprint which has set it up. (A passcode also has to be set up in case the Touch ID does not work.)

Adding a passcode
When the iPad is locked, i.e. the Lock screen is displayed, it can be unlocked simply by swiping on the **slide to unlock** button. However, this is not secure, as anyone could unlock the phone. A more secure option is to add a numerical passcode. To do this:

Tap once on the **Passcode Options** link in Step 3 to access other options for creating a passcode. These include a **Custom Alphanumeric Code**, a **Custom Numeric Code** and a **4-Digit Code**. The 4-Digit Code is the least secure and the Alphanumeric Code is the most secure as it can use a combination of numbers, letters and symbols.

1 Select **Settings > Touch ID & Passcode**

2 Tap on the **Turn Passcode On** button

3 Enter a six-digit passcode. This can be used to unlock your iPad from the Lock screen

4 Tap on the **Require Passcode** button in Step 2 to specify a time period until the passcode is required on the Lock screen. The best option is **Immediately**, otherwise someone else could access your iPad

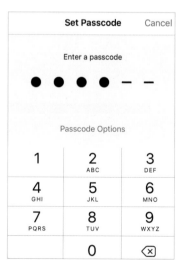

16

Fingerprint sensor with Touch ID

To create a unique fingerprint ID for unlocking your iPad:

1 Select **Settings > Touch ID & Passcode**

2 Create a passcode as shown on the previous page (this is required if the fingerprint sensor is unavailable, or does not work, for any reason)

3 Drag the **iPad Unlock** button to **On**

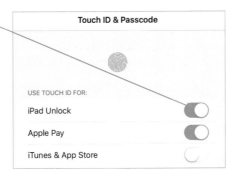

The Touch ID function can also be used with Apple Pay, the Apple contactless payment system that is activated with Touch ID. This has to be set up by adding debit and credit cards and it is more realistic to use it with an iPhone than an iPad.

4 Tap on the **Add a Fingerprint...** link. This presents a screen for creating your Touch ID

FINGERPRINTS

Add a Fingerprint...

5 Place your finger on the Home button several times until the Touch ID is created. This will include capturing the edges of your finger. The screens move automatically after each part is captured and the fingerprint icon turns red

Cancel

Place Your Finger

Lift and rest your finger on the Home button repeatedly.

Several fingerprints can be added for the Touch ID function. It is a good idea to add at least one for each hand so that you can always unlock your iPad, even if you are using one hand for another task.

17

Find My iPad

Losing an iPad that is used in the workplace (or having it stolen) can cause considerable problems for both the individual involved and the organization. However, the Find My iPad function (operated through the iCloud service) allows you to locate a missing device, send a message and an alert, and also remotely lock it or even wipe its contents. This gives added peace of mind, knowing that even if your iPad is lost or stolen, its contents will not necessarily be compromised. To set up Find My iPad:

1 Tap on the **Settings** app

2 Tap on the **iCloud** tab

3 Tap on the **Find My iPad** link and drag the button to **On** to be able to find your iPad on a map

Hot tip

Location Services must be turned On to enable the Find My iPad service (**Settings > Privacy** and turn **On Location Services**).

4 Tap on the **Allow** button to enable the Find My iPad functionality

> **Find My iPad**
> This enables Find My iPad features, including the ability to show the location of this iPad on a map.
>
> Cancel   Allow

Finding a lost iPad

Once you have set up Find My iPad you can search for it through the iCloud service. To do this:

Don't forget

When you click on the **Find iPhone** button in Step 2 you have to enter your password again, even though you will have already done this to log in to your iCloud account initially.

1 Log in to your iCloud account at **www.icloud.com**

2 Click on the **Find iPhone** button (this also works for the iPad)

3 Click on the **All Devices** button and select your iPad. It is identified and its current location is displayed on the map

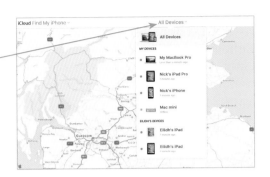

4 Click on the green circle to view details about when your iPad was located

5 Click here to send a sound alert to your iPad

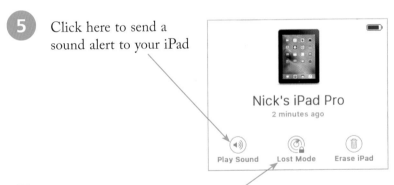

6 Click here to lock your iPad

7 Enter a passcode (including a 6-digit passcode, see tip on page 16) so that no-one else can access the contents on your iPad

Beware

If you lose an iPad containing business documents, or if it is stolen, report it to your manager immediately, even if you have disabled it with Lost Mode in Find My iPad.

Don't forget

Click once on the **Erase iPad** button in Step 5 to delete the iPad's contents.

19

Network Connections

Wi-Fi

Connecting to the internet via Wi-Fi is a standard part of life for most computer users these days, and for anyone in a working environment it is usually essential. It can be used for connecting to the web for research and communication, using email, and accessing online cloud storage services in order to save, back up, access and share documents. To connect to the internet using Wi-Fi on an iPad:

If you are connecting your iPad to the internet via Wi-Fi in your workplace, check the details with your IT Administrator first.

1 Tap on the **Settings** app and tap on the **Wi-Fi** tab

2 Drag the **Wi-Fi** button to **On**

Once a network has been joined, a tick appears next to it, indicating it is the active Wi-Fi connection.

✓ PlusnetWireless792287

3 Tap on a network to select it and enter the password for your Wi-Fi router. Tap on the **Join** button

VPN

VPN stands for Virtual Private Network and this is a method of network connection that is used by businesses so that their employees can log in to the office network over the internet, from remote locations. To connect to a VPN network:

Since a VPN connection involves logging in over the internet, there are a number of security issues that an organization has to consider when using VPN. Because of this, you should discuss joining a VPN network with your IT Administrator, who will also be able to provide you with the required settings.

1 Select **Settings > General** and tap on the **VPN** button

VPN   Not Connected >

2 Tap on the **Add VPN Configuration...** button

3 Enter the configuration settings provided by your IT Administrator

Drawing with the Apple Pencil

The Apple Pencil is the ideal device for drawing on the iPad using a drawing or design app. Look for ones that have been specifically enhanced for the Apple Pencil to utilize its full potential (the app details in the App Store should state if an app has been optimized for the Apple Pencil). If an app is not optimized for the Apple Pencil you will still be able to draw with it, but for apps that have been enhanced for the Apple Pencil you will also be able to:

- Change line thickness by altering the pressure with which you are drawing. A light pressure creates a thin line and applying more pressure creates a thicker line.

- Add shading by tilting the head of the Apple Pencil so that it is at an angle.

Palm rejection

The technology within the Apple Pencil enables the iPad Pro to detect when you are using your finger on the touchscreen, or the Apple Pencil. The user does not need to do anything; the iPad Pro works it out and amends the touchscreen accordingly.

One of the benefits of the Apple Pencil is that the iPad Pro uses palm rejection technology when it identifies that the Apple Pencil is being used. This means that you can rest your hand on the screen while you are drawing or writing with the Apple Pencil and nothing will be activated: you can work in the same way as if you are writing or drawing on paper.

Despite its length, the Apple Pencil has an excellent feel to it and feels very natural when drawing or writing.

Some apps that are optimized for use with the Apple Pencil have a free version that does not include the full functionality: the paid-for version is required for this.

Beware

Although the multitasking options of Slide Over and Split View on the iPad are a good step forward in terms of productivity, they are still some way short of being able to view and work with multiple windows on a desktop computer or a laptop.

Beware

If you tap on the app in the left-hand panel in Slide Over view, this becomes the active app and takes up the whole screen again.

Multitasking

One of the drawbacks of earlier models of iPad, in terms of productivity, was that it was only possible to view one app at a time on the screen. With iOS 9, productivity options are expanded by being able to view two apps at a time on the screen (only with certain models). This means that it can be easier to get tasks done as you can see content from two apps at once.

Slide Over

Slide Over is an option that is available on the iPad Pro, iPad Mini 2 (and later) and iPad Air (and later) and it enables you to access a bar of available apps. To do this:

1 With an app open, swipe inwards from the right-hand edge of the iPad screen

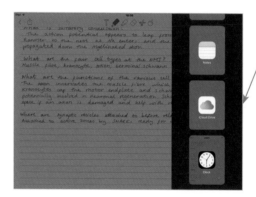

2 Tap on one of the apps in the bar to make it active in the right-hand side of the panel

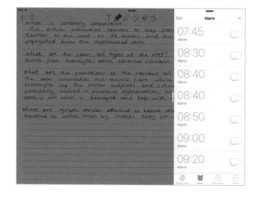

3 Tap on this button to view the Slide Over bar to select another app

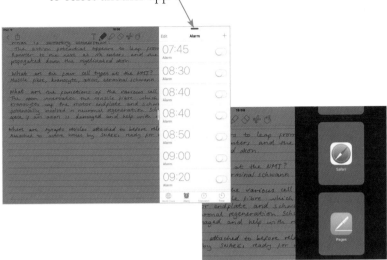

Split View

On the iPad Pro and iPad Air 2 (and later) the concept of Slide Over is taken one step further by Split View: when the second app is active in the right-hand side of the screen (in Split View), drag the left-hand border of the app's window into the middle of the screen. Both open apps will now take up half of the screen and they can be worked on independently of each other.

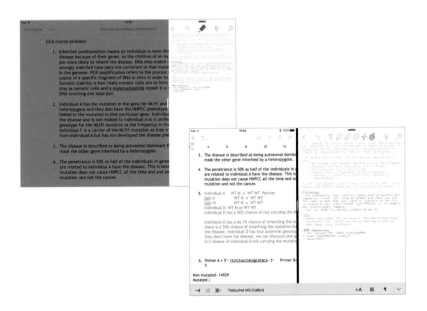

Hot tip

The Picture in Picture function is another multitasking option that enables a FaceTime video to be minimized on the screen, but remain active so that you can still view and perform other tasks at the same time.

31

Don't forget

Drag this button on the middle bar of Split View to change the proportions of each panel. Drag the button to the left or right of the screen to exit Split View and close one of the panels.

Multi-Touch Gestures

Much of the navigation around the iPad screen is done with Multi-Touch Gestures: a range of swipes and taps that access different options. Some of these are:

- Pinch together with thumb and four fingers to return to the Home screen from any open app.

- Double-tap with one finger to zoom in on a web page, photo, map or document. Double-tap with two fingers to return to the original view.

- Swipe outwards with thumb and forefinger to zoom in on a web page, photo, map or document.

- Pinch together with thumb and forefinger to zoom back out on a web page, photo, map or document.

- Swipe left or right with four or five fingers to move between open apps.

- Drag with two or three fingers to move a web page, photo, map or document.

- Press and swipe down on any free area on the screen to access the Spotlight Search box.

- Swipe left or right with one finger to move between full-size photos in the Photos app.

- Tap once on a photo thumbnail with one finger to enlarge it to full screen within the Photos app.

- Drag up from the bottom of the screen to access the Control Center. This contains a range of quick actions including play and volume buttons for music, screen brightness, Airplane Mode, Wi-Fi, Bluetooth, Do Not Disturb and Screen Lock.

- Drag down at the top-middle of the iPad to view current notifications in the Notification Center.

Hot tip

The Spotlight Search box can be used to find items on your iPad, search the web or find nearby businesses and services, such as restaurants and cinemas (Location Services have to be turned **On** for this).

Hot tip

The options for the Notification Center can be set up in the **Settings** app. Tap on the **Notifications** tab and select the items you want to include in the Notification Center.

3 Productivity Apps

For the iPad to be effective in the workplace it has to be able to perform a range of productivity tasks. This chapter looks at the types of apps available for this and how to work with them.

Don't forget

The bottom App Store toolbar is the same for all categories and consists of **Featured**, **Top Charts**, **Explore**, **Purchased** and **Updates**.

Don't forget

Apps can also be searched for using the Search box in the top right-hand corner of the App Store.

Hot tip

To view the top productivity apps, access the Productivity category and tap on the **Top Charts** button on the bottom toolbar.

Top Charts

Accessing Productivity Apps

Since productivity is now a genuine option on the iPad, there is a whole category dedicated to it in the App Store. This contains a wide range of productivity apps that can be downloaded and managed in the same way as for any other apps from the App Store. To access the productivity apps:

1 Tap on the **App Store** app

2 Tap on the **Categories** button

3 Tap on the **Productivity** button

4 The featured productivity apps are displayed

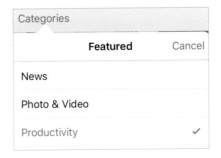

5 Swipe up and down to view all of the featured apps. Tap on the **See All** button next to a section to view its full contents

Installing Apps

Once you have found the productivity apps that you want to use, you can download them to your iPad. To do this:

1 Tap on the **Get** button next to an app

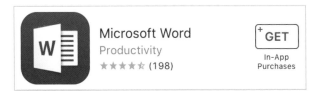

2 Tap on the **Install** button

3 Enter your Apple ID details and tap on the **OK** button

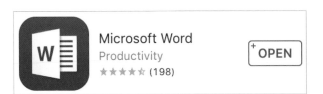

4 Tap on the **Open** button to open the app (or open it by tapping on it on the Home screen)

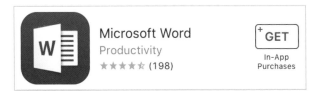

5 Tap on the **Purchased** button to view the apps you have downloaded from the App Store

6 Tap on the **Updates** button to view and install updates for your apps

If an app is a paid-for one, it will have its price in place of the **Get** button in Step 1.

Some apps offer **In-App-Purchases**. This is additional functionality that has to be paid for, even if the app was originally free to download.

To install updates to apps automatically, tap on the **Settings** app and tap on the **iTunes & App Store** tab. Under **Automatic Downloads**, drag the **Updates** button to **On**.

iWork Apps

Apple has its own range of productivity apps that can be used for word processing, spreadsheets and presentations. They are known as the iWork suite of apps and consist of Pages, Numbers and Keynote. These are free to download from the Productivity category of the App Store. To do this:

Each of the iWork apps have to be downloaded separately; they cannot be download in one operation for the whole suite of apps.

Don't forget

For a detailed look at Pages, see Chapter Five; for Numbers, see Chapter Six; for Keynote, see Chapter Seven.

1 Tap on this button on the **Featured** page of the **Productivity** category

2 Tap on the **Get** button for each of the apps

3 Each of the apps have templates from which content can be created and they can also be used with the iCloud Drive to save and share files

Microsoft Office Apps

One of the great advances for productivity on the iPad has been the availability of compatible versions of Microsoft Office apps, including Word, Excel, PowerPoint and OneNote. For many people, these are the apps of choice for productivity tasks, as they are frequently used in working environments. These apps can now be downloaded from the App Store, and various subscription models are available to access their full functionality. To start working with Microsoft Office apps:

1 Access the **Productivity** category of the App Store, as shown on page 34

2 Tap on the **Office** button

3 Tap on one of the apps to view its details

4 Tap on the **Get** button to download the app

The free versions of the Office apps can only be used to view documents. For the full functionality you need to take out a subscription that is renewed monthly. See pages 38-39 for details.

37

When you create a subscription for one of the Office apps, you automatically get access to the others in the suite: the subscription is for Office 365 rather than a specific app.

Opening Office Apps

The versions of the Office apps Word, Excel and PowerPoint are free to download from the App Store, but this only allows you to view documents; you cannot create or edit them. For this necessary functionality you need to create a Microsoft Account and select a subscription model for using the app. To do this:

For a detailed look at Word, see Chapter Five; for Excel, see Chapter Six; for PowerPoint, see Chapter Seven.

1 Tap on one of the Office apps to open it

2 Tap on the **Sign In** button if you already have a Microsoft Account. If not, tap on the **Create an Account** button (an account can be created for free, with an email address and a password)

Office 365

Sign In to Create and Edit Documents

Use your Microsoft account or the work or school account you use to access Office 365

Sign In

Create an Account

Sign In Later ›

3 Once you have a Microsoft Account, enter your email address and tap on the **Next** button

Documents created in Office apps on an iPad can be stored in OneDrive, Microsoft's online storage and sharing service.

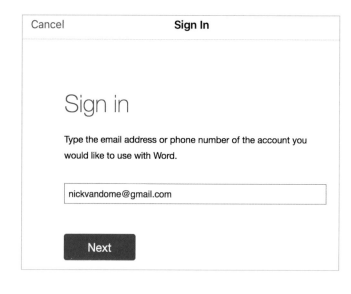

Cancel **Sign In**

Sign in

Type the email address or phone number of the account you would like to use with Word.

nickvandome@gmail.com

Next

4 Enter your Microsoft Account password and tap on the **Sign in** button

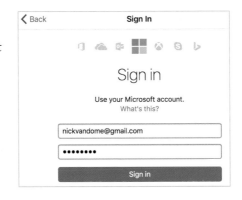

5 By default, you get a free month's trial of the Office apps, which starts once you sign in with your Microsoft Account. Tap on the **Create and Edit** button to start working with the app, or the **Upgrade Now** button to view your subscription details

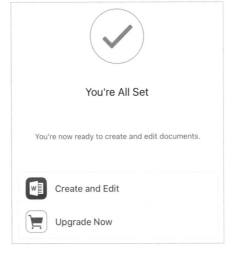

6 Tap on one of the subscription models. This takes you to a sign in page for the iTunes Store. Enter your Apple ID password to start the subscription

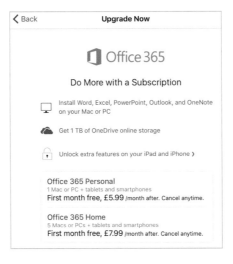

Although the Office apps are Microsoft products, the subscription is paid through your Apple ID account, as the apps are sold through the App Store.

To cancel the Office 365 subscription, tap on the **Settings** app and tap on the **iTunes & App Store** tab. Tap on your **Apple ID** name and tap on **View Apple ID**. Under **Subscriptions**, tap on **Manage**. Tap on the Office app name under **Subscriptions** and drag the **Automatic Renewal** button to **Off**.

Google Productivity Apps

There is a range of Google productivity apps that are similar to the Apple and Microsoft ones in terms of covering word processing, spreadsheets and presentations. The Google versions are Google Docs, Google Sheets and Google Slides and they can all be downloaded from the App Store.

These versions are designed to be used within the cloud, using the Google Drive app. To use this you must have a Google Account, which can be created when you first open one of the apps by entering an email address and a password. Once this has been done, you can starting using the Google productivity apps.

The Google Drive app can also be used to store photos and videos.

Documents created in the Google productivity apps can be shared between different devices without using Google Drive. This gives greater flexibility in terms of accessing them through a browser too.

1   Tap on one of the apps and tap on the **Sign In** button

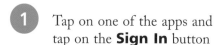

SIGN IN

2   Enter your Google Account email address and tap on the **Next** button

3   Enter your Google Account password and tap on the **Next** button to start using the app

...cont'd

Using Google Drive
While the Google productivity apps can be used on their own they gain additional flexibility if Google Drive is also used for storing your content. To do this:

1 Access **Google Drive** in the **App Store** and download it

2 Tap on the **Google Drive** app to open it

3 Tap on the **Sign In** button to sign in with your Google Account details

4 The **My Drive** folder displays any items that you have created with the Google productivity apps. Tap on an item to open it

5 Tap on this button to create a new folder, upload items into Google Drive (including from your iCloud Drive), take a photo or create a document with one of the Google productivity apps

Hot tip

If you are already signed in to one of the Google productivity apps shown on the previous page, you will not need to enter your sign in details again when you tap on the Google Drive Sign In button.

41

Don't forget

If you try to create a new document with one of the Google apps that you have not downloaded onto your iPad, you will be prompted to do so when you tap on the app in Step 5.

Hot tip

Documents can be shared from Pages, Numbers and Keynote to Google Drive by tapping on the **Share** button and then tapping on the **Open in Another App** button. You will be given the option to copy the document in a different file format, such as PDF, and in some cases the formatting may change when it is uploaded to Google Drive.

Don't forget

If you tap on the **My Drive** button in Step 5 you will be able to specify an existing location into which you want to save the item, or you can create a new folder by tapping on this button at the top of the My Drive window.

...cont'd

Sharing with Google Drive

Once Google Drive has been installed it can be used in conjunction with other apps on your iPad so that you can store content there. To do this:

1 In a compatible app such as Photos, tap on the **Share** button

2 If Google Drive is not showing as one of the options, tap on the **More** button

More

3 Drag the **Google Drive** button to **On**

Google Drive

4 Tap on the **Google Drive** button

Google Drive

5 Tap on the **My Drive** button to select a new location within Google Drive where the item will be saved (by default it is in the main My Drive window). Tap on the **Upload** button to copy the item into your Google Drive

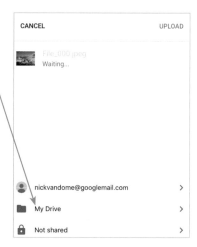

CANCEL   UPLOAD

File_000.jpeg
Waiting...

nickvandome@googlemail.com   >

My Drive   >

Not shared   >

6 The item is uploaded to the selected Google Drive folder

☰ My Drive

Files

CELLS
BASIC UNITS OF LIFE

Collaboration   :   Essay   :   File_000.jpeg

Adobe Apps

Another popular range of productivity apps are those produced by Adobe. These cover topics including photography, design and desktop publishing and are used widely in the creative industries. To use the Adobe apps:

1 Enter **adobe** into the App Store **Search** box

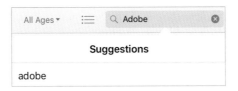

2 Tap on the Adobe apps you want to use, to view their details

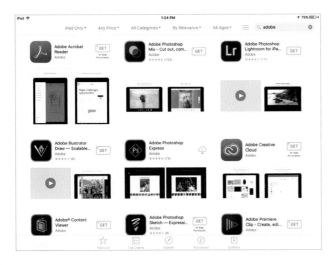

3 Some Adobe apps, such as the **Adobe Creative Cloud** can be used to view and work on documents that you have created with Adobe apps on other devices

The Adobe apps for iPad do not all have the same functionality as the full versions used on desktop computers. However, they are useful for viewing documents and undertaking some editing tasks.

Download the Adobe Acrobat Reader app for viewing PDF documents, and also adding annotations to them and filling-in forms. If you upgrade to Acrobat Pro DC (using In-App Purchases) you will also be able to edit, convert and share PDFs.

Drawing and Design Apps

With the Apple Pencil, the iPad Pro is an ideal device for designers and artists to create engaging content that can be displayed on the iPad, and also shared with colleagues and associates. Even without the Apple Pencil, similar types of content can be produced with the drawing and design apps in the App Store. Some to look at include:

Procreate

A powerful and high-quality drawing app that enables you to create stunning artwork. It includes layers so that you can create different parts of a drawing separately, filters, and thousands of brush types. It is optimized for use with the Apple Pencil.

uMake

This is a 3D sketching app that is useful for designers who want to create detailed 3D versions of their ideas. It is possible to import photos to use as guides for designs and use live-symmetry.

Concepts

Another app for designers or architects, that can be used to create color 3D designs. Up to five layers can be used to build up designs and there is a wide range of vector brush types.

Sketches

Enhanced for use on the iPad Pro with the Apple Pencil, this is a drawing app that includes several layers for each drawing, a brush editor and folders for storing your finished artwork.

Drawing Desk

Another drawing app, which has four different modes, including Sketch Desk and Photo Desk modes. Sketch Desk is the best option for general drawing and it is enhanced for the iPad Pro.

LogoScopic Studio

This is an app for anyone who wants to create corporate logos. It includes 850 logo templates and 100 fonts, so you do not need to have specific design experience to make your own logos.

4 File Management

This chapter looks at how you can arrange and manage your files and folders, using cloud storage services such as iCloud and Dropbox.

About File Management

The iPad operating system, iOS, was not designed with a file management structure, e.g. as with File Explorer for Windows and the Finder for Mac OS X. One of the reasons for this was security, to try to ensure that as few apps as possible had to interact with each other, in case any were infected with viruses. This meant that content created within a certain app could only be accessed from within that app: the apps used a homepage to display documents and folders.

However, as the iPad has become more of a productivity tool the need for some form of file management has increased. Although the options for file management are not as robust as those for desktop or laptop computers, there are now some apps that can perform file management tasks. Some of the options are:

iCloud Drive

This is Apple's own file management app that works with the online iCloud service. It can be used to store and share documents created in the Apple productivity suite, Pages, Numbers and Keynote, and also from other apps that support iCloud Drive, such as the Microsoft suite of Office apps. iCloud Drive has a fairly basic file structure but it does offer a way to store files of different types in different locations.

Cloud apps

Other cloud apps, such as Dropbox, can be used to store documents and then access them from their respective app. Cloud apps usually allow you to create different levels of folders so that you can organize your documents.

File management apps

Within the App Store there is a range of apps that have been designed for file management on the iPad. Most of these operate by connecting to cloud services and enabling you to manage your files from there.

Since the introduction of the iPad Pro, the issue of file management has become more significant and it is an area that is likely to see considerable development, in order to provide the iPad Pro with powerful file management options in the future.

The iPad does not have a Desktop into which documents can be saved, in the way they can on a desktop PC or laptop.

Setting Up iCloud Drive

Managing content via an iPad can be done through the online iCloud service. Within this, iCloud Drive can be used specifically for creating folders for content such as text documents, spreadsheets and presentations. To use iCloud Drive, it first has to be set up:

47

1 In the **iCloud** section of the **Settings** app, tap on the **iCloud Drive** button

2 Drag the **iCloud Drive** button to **On**

3 For the apps you want to use with iCloud Drive, drag these buttons to **On**

4 Tap on the **iCloud Drive** app on the Home screen

5 Tap on one of the folders within iCloud Drive to view its content

Documents are saved into iCloud and the iCloud Drive: iCloud Drive should be seen as more of file management system since it has folders into which specific documents are saved.

iCloud is designed primarily for backing up and sharing content such as photos, email, contacts, calendars, reminders, safari settings and notes. For productivity apps, such as Pages, Numbers and Keynote, iCloud Drive is the best option.

Your iCloud account can be accessed online from www.icloud.com (log in with your Apple ID).

Using iCloud Drive

Once iCloud Drive has been set up it can be used with the compatible apps such as Pages, Numbers and Keynote.

1 Create a document in an app such as Pages

2 Name the document in the **Pages** window (**Project Proposal**)

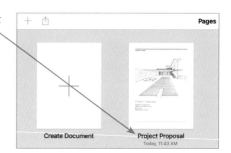

3 Tap on the iCloud Drive app on the Home screen

4 Tap on the relevant folder

5 The newly created document is available in the iCloud Drive folder

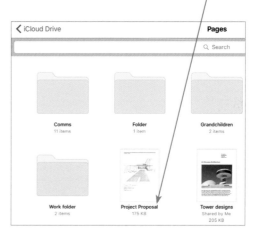

48

Managing iCloud Drive

Although iCloud Drive is not a complex file management system, it does provide some functionality:

1 At the top-level, tap on the **Select** button

2 Tap on the **New Folder** button

3 Enter a name for the new folder (**Reports**) and tap on the **Create** button

New Folder

Enter a name for this folder.

Reports

Cancel   Create

4 The folder is added to the top-level file hierarchy

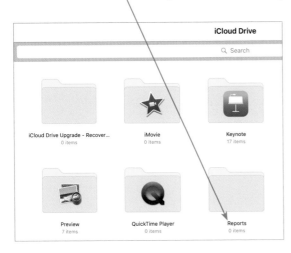

iCloud Drive

Q Search

iCloud Drive Upgrade - Recover...
0 items

iMovie
0 items

Keynote
17 items

Preview
7 items

QuickTime Player
0 items

Reports
0 items

5 Tap on the **Select** button in Step 1 and tap on a folder to select it

Reports
0 items

6 Tap on the **Move** button

Nested folders, i.e. folders within folders, can be created as part of your file structure. To do this, open a folder and follow Steps 1-3.

The main Pages, Numbers and Keynote folders cannot be moved from the top level of the iCloud Drive file structure, i.e. those in the main iCloud Drive window.

To delete a folder, select it as in Step 5 and tap on the **Delete** button.

Multiple folders, or files, can be selected and moved together.

...cont'd

Beware

When moving a folder, its own name will be available in the window in Step 7, as this is where it is in the iCloud Drive file structure. However, it is not possible to move it into its existing location.

7 Tap on the location into which you want to move the folder (**Work Files**)

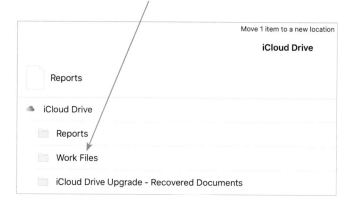

8 Open the top-level folder to check that the other folder has been moved there

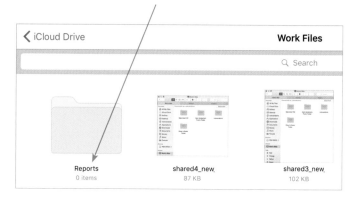

Beware

Sub-folders and files can only be moved within their main, top-level, folder, i.e. you cannot move a spreadsheet from the Numbers folder into the Pages folder.

9 Files can also be moved within individual folders, using the same process

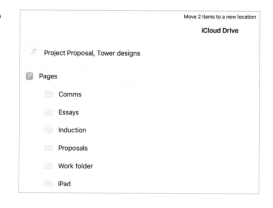

Folders in Dropbox

Dropbox is a cloud storage and backup service that can be used to store your files and documents. Folders and sub-folders can be added to create a file structure. To use Dropbox and create a file structure:

Don't forget

① Download Dropbox from the App Store and tap on its icon

② Tap on the **Files** button

③ Tap on this button to access the Files menu

④ Tap on the **Create Folder** button

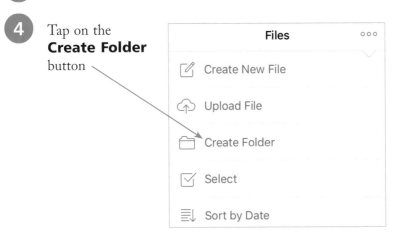

You have to register for Dropbox with a username and password in order to use the service. It is free to do this and you also get 2GB of free storage. More storage can be earned in several ways, including referring friends or colleagues who then register for a Dropbox account.

51

⑤ Give the folder a name and tap on the **Create** button

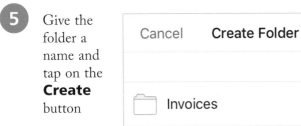

Hot tip

There is a paid-for business option for Dropbox, which can be used with a minimum of five users.

⑥ Open a folder and repeat Steps 3, 4 and 5 to create a sub-folder so that you can start to build up a file structure

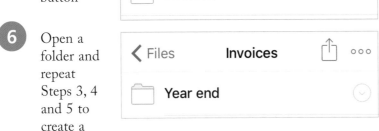

Don't forget

Files in Dropbox can be accessed from any device where you can log in to the Dropbox app or the Dropbox website at www.dropbox.com

Using a File Manager App

File Manager apps from the App Store do not create a file structure in the traditional sense of one on a desktop computer or laptop. However, they can be used to link to online cloud accounts so that you can manage any files that you have here. To do this:

1 Enter File Manager into the App Store Search box and tap on one of the results to download it

File Manager

2 Open the app, then tap on the cloud button to connect to an online cloud service

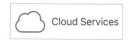

Cloud Services

3 Select the required cloud service

< File Manager

Google Drive

Dropbox

4 Enter your login details for the cloud service

Dropbox   Cancel

File Manager - Cloud and Network File Manager would like access to the files and folders in your Dropbox.

Sign in to Dropbox to link with File Manager - Cloud and Network File Manager

Email

Password

Sign in and Link

5 Once the service is linked to your file manager app you will be able to access the files within it and also the file structure that has been created

< Cloud Services

Invoices

Nick Vandome (1)

Public

52

5 Word Processing

Word processing is one of the foundations of productivity in the workplace, whether it is for reports, proposals, letters or newsletters. This chapter looks at Apple's word processor, Pages, Microsoft Word and Google Docs. For each app there are details about opening and saving documents on the iPad and also adding a range of content, from tables to photos. It also covers sharing documents with colleagues.

Pages: Creating Documents

Pages is Apple's word processing app and it has been developed to a point where it is a realistic option for creating documents in the workplace. The first step in Pages is to create a new document. This can either be a blank template, or one from a template which includes pre-inserted content. To do this:

1 Tap on the **Pages** app

2 Tap on the **Create Document** button

3 Tap on either one of the blank templates for a file with no content, or one with pre-inserted content

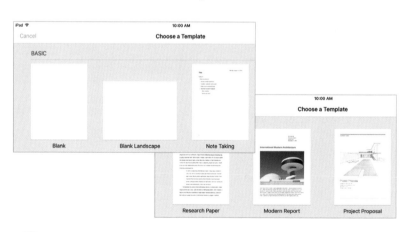

10:01 AM

Modern Report

4 Tap on content to select it and over-write it with your own content

54

Pages: Saving Documents

When a document is created in Pages it is automatically saved within the Pages file structure. From here it can be viewed and renamed. To do this:

1 From within the current document you are working on, tap on the **Documents** button

2 The new document is displayed within the **Pages** window

3 Tap on the document name to select it and access the **Rename Document** window

4 Enter a new name for the document

5 Tap on the **Done** button

6 Tap on the document, or any other in the **Pages** window, to open it

Once a document has been created and saved within Pages, it is also available within the iCloud Drive app and can be accessed from there on other compatible devices. For more information about the iCloud Drive, see Chapter Nine.

Similar types of documents can be grouped together in folders. See page 56 for details.

Pages: Managing Documents

By default, new documents are displayed within the main Pages window, i.e. the top-level. However, it is possible to create folders into which you can put similar documents.

Don't forget

Folders are displayed with a gray background in the Pages window. Individual files are displayed with a white background.

Beware

You can only create one level of folders within Pages; you cannot create 'nested' folders, i.e. folders within folders.

Hot tip

Tap on a folder to open it and then tap on individual files within it to open them. Tap and hold on a file within a folder and drag it away from the folder to remove it from the folder and place it back in the top level of the Pages window.

1 In the **Pages** window, press and hold on a document until all of the documents in the window start to jiggle and the file is selected (indicated by a blue border)

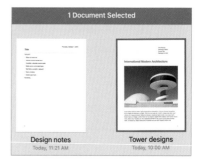

2 Drag the document over another and release it

3 A new folder is created

4 Tap on the folder name and over-write it to create a new name

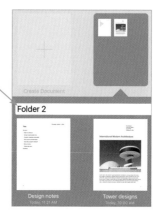

5 Tap on the **Done** button

Editing in the Pages window

Some simple editing can be done to the documents within the Pages window. To do this:

1 Tap on the **Edit** button

2 Tap on a document in the **Select a Document** window to select it (this is indicated by a blue border)

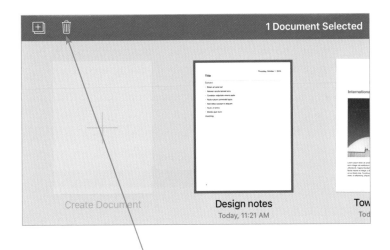

3 Tap on this button and tap on **Delete Document** to delete the selected document(s)

4 Tap on this button to create a copy of the selected document(s)

5 Tap on the **Done** button to return to the main Pages window

Tap on the question mark icon next to the Edit button to view tooltips about the items in the Pages window.

Several documents can be selected at the same time when in the **Select a Document** window, by tapping on each of them, and the same action applied to them.

If you tap on a folder within the **Select a Document** window, it will just open the folder. However, you can then select a document within the folder.

Tap on the **Versions** button (next to the Done button) to view the Version History for a selected document and restore earlier versions.

57

Pages: Working with Text

Once a new document has been created in Pages, content can be added, usually starting with text:

Drag the orange triangle and rectangle on the top ruler to move the margins of the current paragraph. Drag the orange rectangle on its own to change the first-line tab, i.e. the amount the first line is indented in the paragraph.

When a word is selected, the blue handles around it can be dragged to select text to the left or right of it.

The options in Step 3 include: cutting, copying, pasting or deleting the selection; replacing it with another word; looking up a dictionary definition; or copying the text style so that it can be pasted onto other piece of text. It can also be used to add a highlight color to a selection and include a non-printing comment about it.

58

1 Tap on the page and start typing where the cursor appears

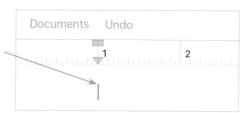

2 Press and hold at the insertion point (where the cursor appears) to access options for selecting text, pasting copied text, highlighting text or adding a comment

3 Double-tap on a word to select it and access the text editing toolbar

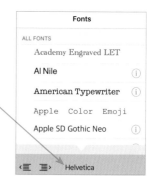

4 Tap on this button on the Shortcuts toolbar to select a specific font

...cont'd

5 Tap on this button on the Shortcuts toolbar to select a font size

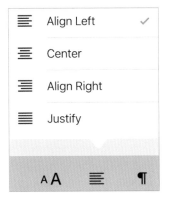

6 Tap on this button on the Shortcuts toolbar to indent the first line of a paragraph

7 Tap on this button on the Shortcuts toolbar to indent or outdent a paragraph

8 Tap on this button to align text

9 Tap on this button to add the required formatting options

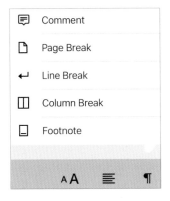

Don't forget

Tap on the Indent button (the right of the two buttons in Step 7) to move a whole paragraph inwards from the left-hand side. Tap again to move it in another step. Tap on the Outdent button to reverse the process.

Don't forget

Page Breaks, Lines Breaks and Column Breaks in Step 9 are non-printing items which means they will not appear in any printed versions.

Don't forget

Since text styles are added at a paragraph level it does not matter where the cursor is inserted in the paragraph. Text styles can also be added to a paragraph when text is selected within the paragraph.

Hot tip

If text selections are made in Step 3 before any text is entered, any subsequent text will display these selections.

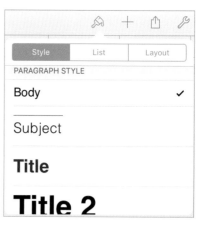

Beware

Text styles default to Helvetica, regardless of what formatting has previously been applied within the paragraph. However, the font for the paragraph, or individual words within it, can be changed after the text style has been applied to the paragraph.

...**cont'd**

Adding text styles

Text styles are preset text formatting groups that can be applied to whole paragraphs of text, so that you do not have to format them manually each time. To add text styles:

1 Tap within a paragraph to insert the cursor or select a piece of text

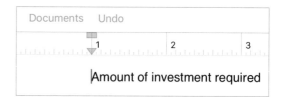

2 Tap on this button on the top toolbar

3 Tap on the font name to select formatting options for the selected text, including size, font and color. Bold, italics, underline, strikethrough and alignment options can also be selected here

4 Tap on a **Paragraph Style** to apply this to the current paragraph

Pages: Adding Graphics

Pages has considerably more functionality than just displaying text and it can also include a variety of graphical elements:

1 Tap on this button on the top toolbar

2 Tap on this button to view the options for adding tables

3 Tap on this button to view options for adding charts

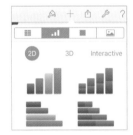

4 Tap on this button to view options for adding objects

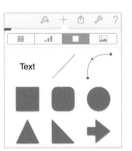

5 Tap on this button to view options for adding photos or videos, either from the Photos app, iCloud Drive or a new one taken with the iPad's camera

Swipe left and right in the panel of each graphical object to view more options. The number of available panels is displayed by the number of dots at the bottom of the panel, and the currently active one is colored orange.

Tap on a graphical element to add it to the current Pages document.

Graphical items, e.g. photos, can be added to cells in a table, as well as text.

...cont'd

Working with graphical elements

Once graphics have been added in Pages they can have content added to them and have their format edited. To do this:

1 Tap on an item to select it. Drag on the resizing handles to change its size

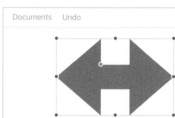

2 For a chart, tap on the chart and tap on the **Edit Data** button to add your own data to the chart

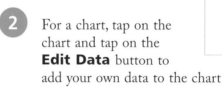

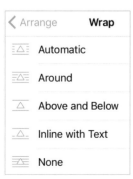
3 Enter data in the **Edit Chart Data** window and tap on the **Done** button

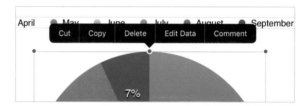

4 Tap on this button on the top toolbar for additional formatting options for the selected item

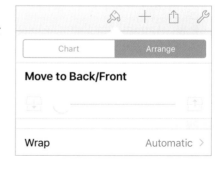

Pages: Settings and Tools

The Settings and Tools menus within Pages provide a range of additional functionality to the app. To use these:

1 Tap on this button on the top toolbar

2 Tap on **Change Tracking** to access options for tracking changes within the document

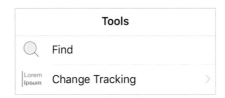

3 Drag the **Tracking** button **On** to display tracking changes in the document. Tap on the **Markup** options that you want to use

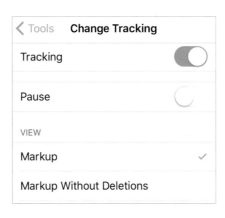

4 Tap on **Document Setup** to access options for adding headers and footers to the document and setting the page margins. Drag on the blue markers further down the page to change the margins

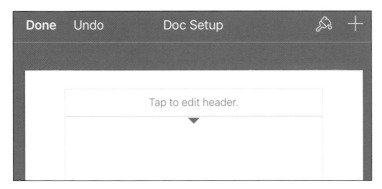

Don't forget

The page in the **Document Setup** window in Step 4 is the document master page. Any changes made here will apply to the whole document. Tap in the header or footer areas to add content here that will appear throughout the document. Tap on this button to add graphical content that will appear at the same point throughout the document.

Hot tip

Press and hold in the header or footer area in Step 4 and tap on **Page Numbers** to access options for applying page numbers automatically throughout the document.

...cont'd

Hot tip

If a word is spelt incorrectly and underlined in red, tap on it and tap on **Replace** to view alternatives.

5 Tap on **Settings** to access a range of settings for the current document. These include: **Check Spelling**, which underlines misspelt words in red; displaying the **Word Count** at the bottom of the document; adding **Comments**; and displaying the **Ruler** at the top of the page. Drag the buttons **On** or **Off** as required

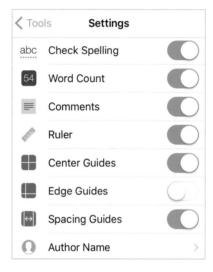

Beware

If you use password protection for any of your Pages documents, make a note of the password and keep this separately from your iPad. If you forget the password you may not be able to access the document again.

6 Tap on **Set Password** to protect the document with a password. Enter the password, verify it and tap on the **Done** button

Cancel	Set Password	Done
	Require a password to open this document:	
Password	••••••••	
Verify	••••••••	
Hint	Red car	

Pages: Exporting Documents

By default, Pages documents are automatically saved within the Documents window and also saved into the iCloud Drive, if set up. This retains them in the Pages document format, which is not compatible with all word processing apps. Therefore, if you want to share a Pages document with someone using another word processing app, it is a good idea to export it into another file format. To do this:

1 Tap on this button on the top toolbar

2 Tap on **Send a Copy** to select a format for sending the document

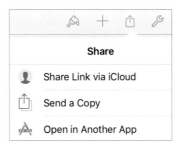

3 Tap on the format into which you want to copy the document (this can also be in Pages format if you want to send it to someone else using the Pages app)

4 Select an option for how you would like to send the newly created document. (Tap on the **Send to** button to copy it to your iCloud Drive)

Some word processing apps can open Pages documents, while others cannot. If you create a copy in other formats, then it will be easier to share the document.

If you are copying a document to your iCloud Drive, tap on the folder into which you want to copy the document and tap on **Export to this location**. Open iCloud Drive to view the newly created document, in the new file format and in the original Pages format.

Pages: Sharing Documents

Sharing documents in the workplace is important, not only to let people read what you have produced, but also to give colleagues the chance to add to, or amend, your original work. One way to do this is to send it to them via email, but a better way is to share it in a collaborative environment. This way, one person or more can make changes to a document while keeping it in the same location. To do this with Pages:

Always make sure that you know which version of a document you are working on.

66

1 Tap on this button on the top toolbar

2 Tap on **Share Link via iCloud**

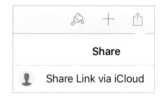

3 In the **Share via iCloud** window, select whether you want the recipient(s) to be able to edit the document or just view it

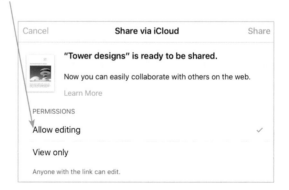

Links to shared documents can also be sent via Twitter and Facebook.

4 Tap on the **Share** button   Share

5 Select how you would like to send the link to the shared document (usually either Message or Mail)

6 Enter the recipient(s) in the selected app and tap on the **Send** button

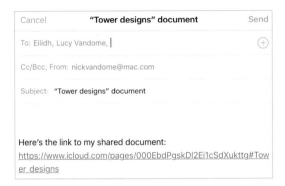

7 Tap on the **Done** button in the **Share via iCloud** window

Working with shared documents

After a document has been shared it can still have its settings amended. To do this:

1 When a document is being shared, this icon replaces the one in Step 1 on the previous page in the top toolbar

2 Tap on **View Share Settings...**

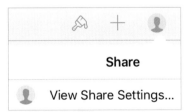

3 The **Share via iCloud** window in Step 3 on the previous page is displayed and the document can be shared again, if required

4 Tap on **Stop Sharing** to disable the sharing function for the current document

Don't forget

When someone receives a link for a shared document, they can use it to access the document online via Apple's iCloud service. The document can then be edited through a Mac browser using OS X, or a PC browser using Windows. When changes are made to the shared document, these changes are automatically applied to the original. The document can also be viewed and downloaded from the link. However, if it is downloaded then changes cannot be made in a collaborative environment.

Beware

Shared documents can be viewed on an iPad but not edited (unless they are downloaded). Editing has to be done via a desktop browser.

Word: Creating Documents

Once Word has been downloaded and set up (see pages 37-39) it can be used to create documents. To do this:

Don't forget

When a new document is created, it is given the name **Document** with a sequential number, e.g. Document1, Document2.

1 Tap on the **Word** app

2 Tap on the **New** button in the left-hand panel

3 Tap on one of the templates (or **Blank Document** to create a document with no content)

Hot tip

Tap on the **Recent** button in the left-hand panel to view the most recent documents that have been created.

4 The document is created based on the selected template

Word: Adding Content

In a new document, content can be added to a blank document or to a preformatted template:

1 Tap on a blank document and start typing text. Tap on the **Home** button to access the formatting tools

Home

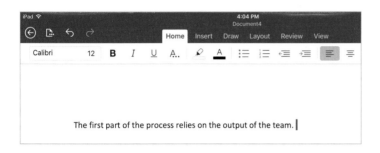

The area above the text in a blank document is the header that appears at the top of every page.

2 In a document based on a preformatted template, tap on one of the placeholders to add text

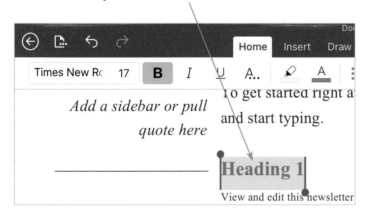

In a document based on a preformatted template, tap on an image to replace it with a picture of your own.

3 Over-write the existing text in a placeholder

Opening Statement

View and edit this newsletter in Word on

Word: Saving Documents

Documents in Word can be saved manually, and there is also an AutoSave function so that you do not have to worry about saving your documents at regular intervals. To save Word documents:

The default locations for saving documents are within your OneDrive folder (this is created when you first create a Microsoft Account) or in the Word app on your iPad. For sharing purposes, it is best to save it into OneDrive or your iCloud Drive, see second tip below.

Tap on the **Add a Place** button in Step 4 to select another cloud service into which you can save the document (such as Dropbox).

Tap on the **More** button in Step 4 to save the document into your iCloud Drive.

70

1 Tap on this button on the top Word toolbar

2 Drag the **AutoSave** button to **On** to ensure the document is automatically saved at regular intervals

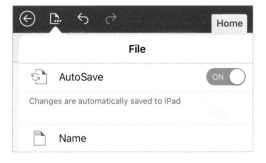

3 Tap on the **Name** button to give the document a unique name

4 Select a location for where you want to save the document

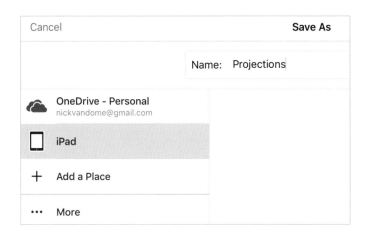

5 Give the document a new name and tap on the **Save** button

Word: Opening Documents

Documents can be opened from the locations into which they were saved, from the main Word window. To do this:

1 From within a document, tap on this button on the top toolbar to access the main window

2 Tap on the **Open** button

3 Select a location from where you want to open a document. Tap on a document to open it

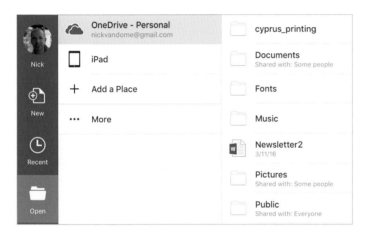

4 If the document is stored in a cloud service, it will be downloaded and opened on your iPad

Hot tip

Once a document has been opened, it can be copied by tapping on the button in Step 1 on the previous page and tapping on the **Duplicate** button. The duplicate can then be saved into a different location from the original, if required.

Word: The Ribbon

In Windows terminology, the collection of tools at the top of Office apps is known as the Ribbon. This is the case in Word, including the iPad version. There are several elements to the Ribbon, each accessed from a button on the top toolbar. To work with the Ribbon:

Home

This contains several options for formatting text:

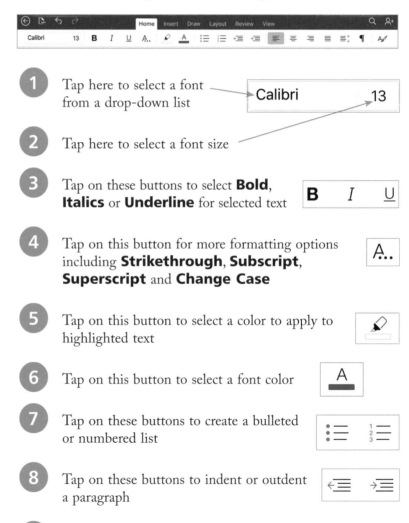

1 Tap here to select a font from a drop-down list — Calibri 13

2 Tap here to select a font size

3 Tap on these buttons to select **Bold**, **Italics** or **Underline** for selected text — **B** *I* U

4 Tap on this button for more formatting options including **Strikethrough**, **Subscript**, **Superscript** and **Change Case** — A...

5 Tap on this button to select a color to apply to highlighted text

6 Tap on this button to select a font color — A

7 Tap on these buttons to create a bulleted or numbered list

8 Tap on these buttons to indent or outdent a paragraph

9 Tap on these buttons to align text (the button on the far right is to adjust line spacing)

Don't forget

Tap on the toolbar headings, e.g. **Home**, **Insert**, etc. to show or hide the Ribbon options.

Don't forget

If text is selected, by double-tapping on it, formatting options will be applied to the selected text. If no selection is made each formatting option will be applied to any text that is then added, until the options are turned off by tapping on their button on the toolbar.

Don't forget

The highlight color in Step 5 adds a colored box around the selected text, it does not change the font color.

10   Tap on this button to Show or Hide non-printing characters, such as word spaces and paragraph returns

11   Tap on this button to select text styles

Insert

This contains options for adding a range of content:

1   Tap on this button to add a new page. This is inserted after the point in the current page where the cursor is located

2   Tap on this button to insert a table. This automatically activates the Table toolbar for formatting and managing tables, including options for inserting rows and columns and style options

3   Tap on this button to add photos from the **Photos** app. This automatically activates the **Picture** toolbar for formatting photos, including options for applying drop shadows, reflections, wrapping text and cropping

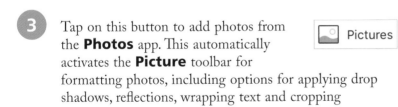

4   Tap on this button to add a photo taken with the camera on your iPad

Hot tip

Showing the non-printing characters can be a good way to view the formatting of a document in terms of paragraph breaks and items such as anchors for photos or shapes.

Don't forget

If the cursor is placed in the middle of a paragraph and a new page is added, the text after the cursor will be place on another page, after the new page, which will be blank.

...cont'd

Hot tip

Once items such as photos and shapes have been added, their toolbars can be activated by tapping on the photo or shape to select them. If they are not selected, their toolbars will not be available.

Don't forget

Hyperlinks appear underlined in a Word document and they can have different display text to the actual web address or email.

Don't forget

Headers and footers can be different on the first page to the rest of the document and also different on odd and even pages. They are best aligned to the left, middle or right.

5 Tap on this button to add shapes and lines to the current document. This automatically activates the **Shape** toolbar for formatting shapes, including adding more shapes, selecting shape styles and fill and outline colors

6 Tap on this button to add a text box

7 Tap on this button to add a hyperlink, to a website or an email address

8 Tap on this button to add a comment to the document

9 Tap on this button to edit, or remove, the headers and footers in the document

10 Tap on this button to add and format page numbers

11 Tap on this button to add a footnote on a page

Ab¹

12 Tap on this button and tap on **See All** to view add-ins for Word (and other Office apps). This includes items such as dictionaries and Wikipedia, which can be used as tools within Word. Tap on an item to download it

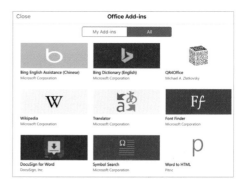

Draw

This contains options for drawing within Word documents:

1. Tap this button **On** to enable drawing on the screen with your finger, or the Apple Pencil

2. Tap on these buttons to select a pen style for drawing in the document

Hot tip

The pen tool on the right in Step 2 can be used to create translucent lines so that some of the background is visible behind.

3. Tap on these buttons to select a line thickness for the selected pen style

4. Tap on these buttons to select a color for the selected pen style

75

5. Tap on this button to access the color wheel to select different colors

6. Swipe around the color wheel to spin it, and tap on a color to make it the currently active one

Beware

When you use the Eraser tool in Step 6, this removes the whole of a drawing segment: you can not erase part of a drawing segment.

7. Tap on this button (Eraser tool) and tap on a drawing in the document to erase it

...cont'd

Layout

This contains options for the layout of the pages in the document:

Hot tip

If you add a Next Page Section Break you will be able to select a different orientation for each page, e.g. portrait for one and landscape for another.

1 Tap on this button to select the direction of text within a table cell

2 Tap on this button to select the margins for the document

3 Tap on this button to select the orientation for the pages in the document

4 Tap on this button to select the paper size for the document

Don't forget

Using columns is a good option when creating newsletters, although there is also a newsletter template that can be used when creating new documents.

5 Tap on this button to add columns to the document

6 Tap on this button to add breaks within the document

Review

This contains options for checking various aspects of text:

① Tap on this button to select a proofing language for the document and turn **On** or **Off** the spell checking facility

② Tap on this button to show the word count, number of pages and number of characters for the document

③ Tap on these buttons to, from left to right, add a comment, delete a comment, move to the previous comment, and move to the next comment

④ Drag this button to **On** to view changes that have been made in a document

⑤ Tap on this button to show the markup for review

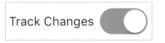

⑥ Tap on these buttons to, from left to right, accept editing changes, reject editing changes, move to the previous comment or tracked change, and move to the next comment or tracked change

Don't forget

Track Changes is usually used for editing purposes when more than one person is working on, or reviewing, a document.

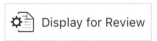

Don't forget

Markup is how editing changes are shown in a document.

Don't forget

If you are a reviewing a document you can accept individual changes, accept all changes or accept all shown changes.

...cont'd

View

This contains options for how you view the current page in the document window:

① Drag this button **On** or **Off** to display the ruler at the top of the document window

② Tap on this button to show a whole page in the document window

③ Tap on this button to fit the page width to the whole document window

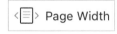

Word: Sharing Documents

Documents can be shared from within the Word app in a number of different ways:

1 Tap on this button to share a document

2 Tap on the **Invite People** option

3 Enter names or email addresses for people with whom you want to share the document. Tap on the **Send** button to send the recipient a link to the document

4 Tap on the **Send Attachment** option in Step 2 to attach the document to an email

5 Select whether to send the document in its Word format or as a PDF file

6 Tap on the **Send a Copy** button

7 Tap on the **Mail** button to attach the document to an email

Beware

Documents have to be saved into a cloud service in order to be able to invite people to share them.

Hot tip

Select a piece of text and tap on the **Copy Link** option in Step 2 to copy a link which can then be pasted into an email, so the recipient has a link with which to view the document.

Don't forget

If you enter names in Step 3, Word will ask to access the Contacts app, to assign email addresses for the named people.

Beware

A document can be attached to a text message in the Message app, but this may create too large a message size.

Google Docs

Another good productivity option, along with Pages and Word, is Google Docs. This is essentially an online word processing app that can be used to create documents that are stored in the cloud (in this case Google Drive) and accessed from other devices using the Google Docs app. To use it on your iPad:

Don't forget

If you have installed Google Drive on your iPad, any documents created in Google Docs will be available here.

1 Enter **Google Docs** into the **App Store** Search box

2 Tap on the **Get** button and then the **Install** button to download **Google Docs**

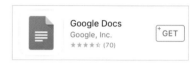

Google Docs
Google, Inc.
★★★★☆ (70)
GET

3 Tap on the **Google Docs** app to open it

Docs

4 Tap on the **Sign In** button

SIGN IN

Don't forget

Once you have signed in to Google Docs you do not have to sign in again if you close the app and re-open it.

5 Enter your Google Account details to sign in (as shown on page 40)

nickvandome@gmail.com

Password
••••••••

Forgot password?   NEXT

80

6 Tap on this icon to create a new document

+

Hot tip

You can view your Google Docs documents online from any browser, by signing in to your Google Account.

7 Tap on either the **Choose template** or **New document** buttons

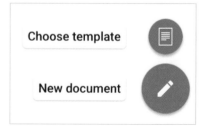

Choose template

New document

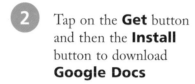

8 For a document based on a template, tap on a template style to create a document with the selected formatting

Google Docs documents that are created from a template are given the default name of the template on which they are based.

9 For a new document, give it a name and tap on the **Create** button

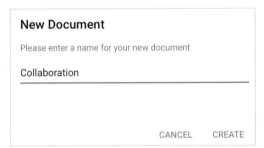

New Document

Please enter a name for your new document

Collaboration

CANCEL   CREATE

The content in a document based on a Google Docs template can all be replaced and over-written with your own text and images.

10 The document is created in the Google Docs window. Tap on this button to save changes to a document

...cont'd

Getting around Google Docs

Within Google Docs there are options for managing your account and also the documents within it:

Don't forget

A document's menu has options for the **Print layout** of the document, **Find and replace...**, **Word count**, **Print preview**, document **Details** and **Share & export** options.

82

Beware

If a document has a pin symbol next to it, this indicates that it is available offline, so it can be edited even when there is no internet connection. If documents are not available offline then you will not be able to access them if you are not connected to the internet (since they are stored online in the Google Drive).

1 From within an open document, tap on this button to edit it

2 Tap on this button to access the menu for the current document

3 Tap on this button to save any changes ✓

4 Tap on this button to move back up to the main Google Docs window

5 The main Google Docs window displays your documents

6 Tap on this button next to a document to access its menu

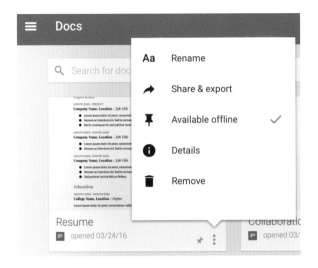

Tap on the **Share & export** button in Step 6 to share the document with other people, send a copy of it, print it, save a copy as a Word document, make a copy of it, or copy a link to your clipboard, which can then be pasted into an email.

83

7 Tap on this button to access the main Google Docs menu

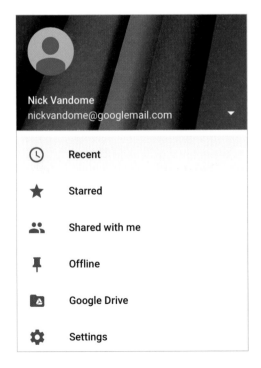

If a document is edited while you are offline, the changes will be applied to the online version the next time you connect to the internet.

The menu in Step 7 is linked to your Google Account. Selections that are made here can be applied across your account, such as those for **Settings**.

...cont'd

8 Tap on these buttons to display the current documents in a list or a grid

9 Tap on this button to view all of the documents in your **My Drive** folder. Tap on an item to open it

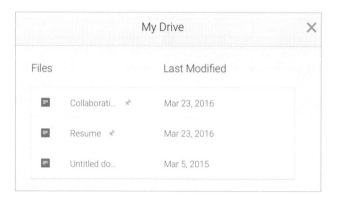

Don't forget

If Google Docs documents are added to your Google Drive on another device they will show up in the **My Drive** folder in Step 9.

My Drive ✕

Files	Last Modified
Collaborati...	Mar 23, 2016
Resume	Mar 23, 2016
Untitled do...	Mar 5, 2015

Editing documents

When working on a document in Google Docs there are a range of editing and formatting options:

Beware

Try to avoid using underlining in documents as it could be confused with a hyperlink for a web or email address.

1 Tap on this button to edit a document

2 Tap on these buttons to add **Bold**, **Italics** or **Underlining** to selected text

B *I* <u>U</u>

3 Tap on these buttons to align text to the **Left** or **Center**

4 Tap on these buttons to add **Numbered** or **Bulleted lists**

5 Tap on these buttons to **Indent** or **Outdent** paragraphs

6 Tap on this button on the top toolbar to access the **Insert** menu

7 Select one of the options to insert content into the document, including **Links** for web pages or email addresses, **Comments**, **Images**, **Tables** and **Horizontal lines**

8 Tap on this button on the top toolbar to access the **Text** menu

9 Select options for formatting text, such as **Style**, **Font**, **Size** and **Text color**

10 Tap on the **Paragraph** tab to access paragraph formatting options

Once objects such as tables and images have been inserted into a document they can be selected by tapping on them, which brings up their own toolbar for editing the item.

Tap on the **Style** button in Step 9 to apply pre-set styles to paragraphs or selected items of text.

Tap on these buttons on the top toolbar to **Undo** or **Redo** previous actions.

Word Processing Apps

There is a wide range of word processing apps in the App Store, covering a range of functionality and price. Depending on what you want to use them for, some may better suit your needs than others. Some to look at include:

Textilus

A versatile word processing app that can be used for creating a wide range of documents in the workplace. Nested folder structures can be created for managing documents, and it also syncs with iCloud and Dropbox.

Werdsmith

This is an app aimed at dedicated writers, and it contains customized fonts and themes. It does not have the same functionality in terms of adding different types of content as some other apps, but there are features for backing up and sharing.

Hanx Writer

This is the app for anyone who yearns for the days of old fashioned, manual typewriters. It offers different styles of typewriter that recreate the sounds and look of a manual machine, while retaining the functionality of a touchscreen device, such as being able to select a word by double-tapping on it.

UX Write

This is a word processing app designed for the workplace, with an emphasis on writing long documents such as reports and research papers. It can also be used to create HTML documents for use on the web.

Glyphic

This is a stylish word processing app that can open a wide range of document formats, and has powerful layout and printing features. It is a paid-for app and this includes some powerful formatting tools, including working with images to make them as elegant as possible.

The Notes app on the iPad is not a word processor but it is a useful tool for taking notes that include bulleted lists and images.

Don't forget

Word processing apps can often be bought in bundles with other productivity apps.

Beware

Some word processing apps have In-App Purchases, where there is a fee for accessing additional functionality for the app.

6 Spreadsheets

Spreadsheets are sometimes seen as the less-glamorous side of productivity in the workplace. However, they are important for a range of tasks; from creating lists, to performing complex financial calculations. This chapter looks at Apple's spreadsheet app, Numbers, Microsoft Excel, and Google Sheets. For each app, there are details about creating spreadsheets and working with items such as formulas, charts and graphs, and formatting in cells.

Numbers: Creating Spreadsheets

Numbers is Apple's spreadsheet app that can be used for entering data, creating charts and graphs and conducting a range of calculations through the inclusion of formulas. To start creating a spreadsheet with Numbers:

Don't forget

Numbers is not a built-in app, but it can be downloaded for free from the App Store.

1 Tap on the **Numbers** app

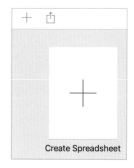

2 Tap on the **Create Spreadsheet** button

3 Tap on either one of the blank templates for a file with no content, or one with pre-inserted content

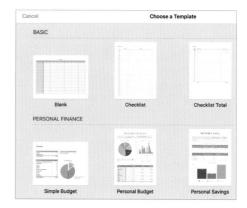

Hot tip

Tap on the **Spreadsheets** button in the top left-hand side of the window to access the main Numbers window, if it is not displayed, for creating a new spreadsheet.

Spreadsheets

4 For a spreadsheet with pre-inserted content, tap on the content to select it and over-write it with your own data

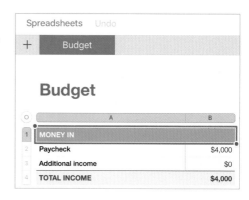

Numbers: Saving Spreadsheets

When a spreadsheet is created in Numbers it is automatically saved within the Numbers file structure. From here it can be viewed and renamed. To do this:

1 From within the current spreadsheet you are working on, tap on the **Spreadsheets** button

2 The new spreadsheet is displayed within the **Numbers** window

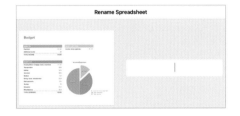

3 Tap on the spreadsheet name to select it and access the **Rename Spreadsheet** window

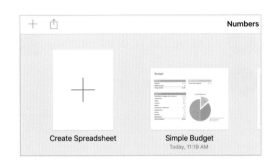

4 Enter a new name for the spreadsheet

First quarter

5 Tap on the **Done** button

Done

6 Tap on the spreadsheet, or any other in the **Numbers** window, to open it

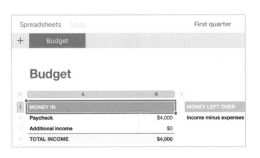

The default name for a new spreadsheet is the one used for its original template in Step 3 on the previous page. If more than one spreadsheet is created from the same template without renaming the previous one(s), each new spreadsheet will have the same name but with an incremental number added to the file name for identification, e.g. Simple Budget and Simple Budget 2.

Tap on this button next to the spreadsheet name to add a new sheet within the current spreadsheet.

Numbers: Adding Tables

Tables are the backbone of spreadsheets and although other types of objects can also be added, this is main type of object with which you will be working in Numbers. To add tables:

Hot tip

To delete the default table, or any other table, tap on the table, tap on this button and tap on the **Delete** button.

Don't forget

Swipe left and right in the Tables panel to view more layout options.

Don't forget

New tables are inserted with a **Table Name** and also **Header** and **Footer** regions. Tap on this button on the top toolbar and tap on the **Headers** button to access options for formatting the headers and footers.

1 By default, a blank spreadsheet opens with a table already pre-inserted

2 Tap on this button on the top toolbar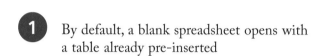

3 Tap on the **Tables** button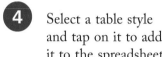

4 Select a table style and tap on it to add it to the spreadsheet

6 If you edit the source data, the chart will be amended accordingly

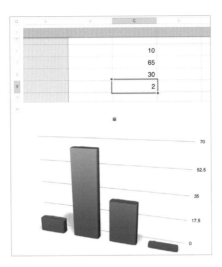

Pie charts can also be created in 2D and 3D, as well as bar charts.

7 Tap on the chart to select it.
Press and hold on it to drag it into a new position

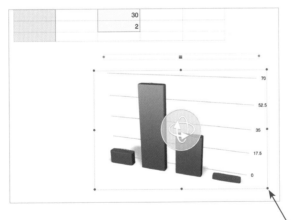

8 Drag the resizing handles around the border to increase or decrease the size of the table

9 Tap on this button to access the chart's toolbar

10 Tap on the **Edit References** button to add more data ranges to the chart

To add a new data range, i.e. another set of data, tap on the **Edit References** button and select a new range of cells in the original table, in Step 1. Enter data into the new selection. This will create a new data range in the chart, denoted with a different color to the first range.

| Cut | Copy | Delete | Edit References | Comment |

Numbers: Designing in Cells

The default layout of tables in a spreadsheet does not particularly lend itself to effective visual designs: its uniformity can be limiting in terms of design. However, there are some ways in which the table layout can be modified to accommodate better text design:

To unmerge (split) a cell that has previously been merged, tap on it once to select it, tap on it again to access the toolbar and then tap on the **Unmerge** button.

1 Tap on the top of a column and drag here to widen a column to fit more text on one line

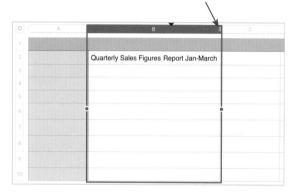

2 For items such as a main heading, tap on the first cell that you want to use and drag over subsequent cells

3 Tap on the **Merge** button 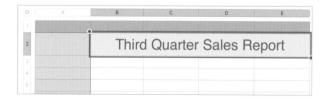 Merge

Merging cells is a good way to create more complex designs within tables.

4 The merged cells span the width of those below it

5 Format the merged cells accordingly for their content

Numbers: Settings and Tools

Numbers has some tools and settings that can be applied to spreadsheets that have been created. To use these:

1 Tap on this button on the top toolbar

2 Tap on options for finding text within a spreadsheet, Settings, setting a password to protect the spreadsheet, printing the spreadsheet and the Numbers Help options

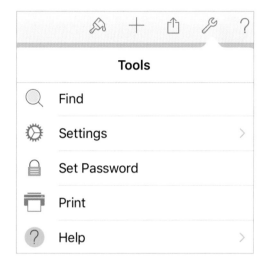

3 Tap on the **Settings** button above, for options to **Check Spelling** in a spreadsheet, add **Comments** and turn **Guides** On or Off, for positioning objects

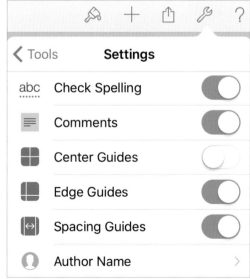

The processes for exporting and sharing spreadsheets in Numbers are the same as for documents in Pages. See pages 66-67 for details.

If objects have been added to a spreadsheet, they can be positioned with great accuracy using the Guides. The Guides show the edges and center of an object while it is being moved, so it can be positioned relative to other objects. **Spacing Guides** can be used to show when three or more objects have the same space between them when they are aligned horizontally or vertically.

Excel: Creating Spreadsheets

Microsoft Excel is part of the Office suite of productivity apps which can be downloaded and opened as shown on pages 37-39. Once this has been done, Excel can be used to create spreadsheets:

1 Tap on the **Excel** app

2 Tap on the **New** button in the left-hand panel

3 Tap on one of the templates (including **Blank Workbook** to create a spreadsheet with no content)

4 The spreadsheet is created based on the selected template

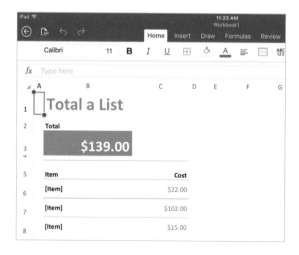

Excel: Adding Content

Excel spreadsheets consist of tables and cells, into which content can be added and functions applied to them, if required. To add content into an Excel spreadsheet on your iPad:

1 Tap on a cell to select it and show its table reference, e.g. C3

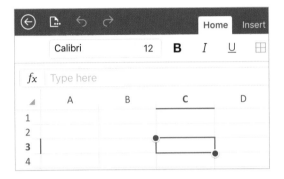

Cell references are used when a formula is added to a cell to create a calculation, e.g. C2xD4. The result is displayed in the cell into which the formula is entered. See page 116 for details.

2 Double-tap on the cell to access the cell input tools, and tap on the **Home** tab

Text and numbers/symbols are the only items that can be added to cells from the Home tab in Step 2. However, other content can be added from the **Insert** tab. See page 113-115 for details.

3 If not already selected, tap on this button to add text to the cell. The equivalent keyboard is accessed

...cont'd

4 Tap on this button to add numbers to the cell. The equivalent keyboard is accessed

Mathematical symbols can also be inserted into the input field.

Tap on the red circle with the white cross to reject an item in the input box.

5 Enter the content in the top input box and tap on this button to apply it

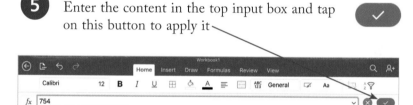

6 Double-tap on a cell to view its content in the editing window and amend it if required

If a cell contains a function or formula, i.e. a calculation of some kind, the cell in the table will display different content from the item in the input box in the editing window. The cell will display the result of the function in the input box, so if the function changes, the result in the cell will change too.

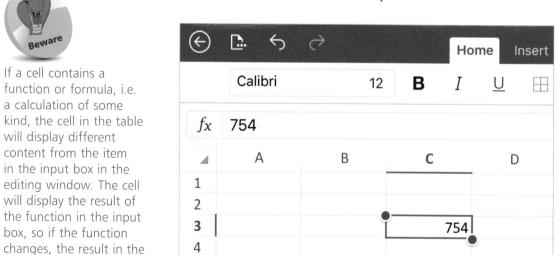

Excel: Working with Cells

Cells in a table can be formatted using the toolbar, accessed from the Home tab of the Ribbon:

1   Tap on a cell to select it and tap on the **Home** tab

2   Tap on this button to select a font

3   Tap on this button to select a font size

4   Tap on these buttons to select **Bold**, **Italics** or **Underline** for selected text

B   *I*   U

5   Tap on this button to select borders for the selected cell

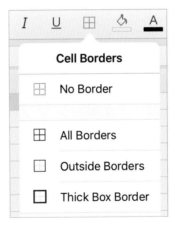

6   Tap on this button to select a fill color for the cell

7   Tap on this button to select a font color

8   Tap on this button to align content in the cell

The formatting is applied to the cell, not the content within it. If the content is edited it will retain the same formatting applied to the cell.

The **Insert** tab on the Ribbon is looked at on page 113-115 and the **Formulas** tab is looked at on pages 116-117. The other tabs are: **Draw**, for creating drawing objects in spreadsheets; **Review**, for adding and viewing comments; and **View** for showing or hiding the Formula Bar, Gridlines, Headings and Sheet Tabs.

...cont'd

The options from Step 10 enable you to select properties for a number format such as number of decimal places, currency symbol, date format and fraction format.

The **Cell Styles** in Step 11 apply groups of formatting styles to the cell, e.g. cell background color and text color. Select one of the themed Cell Styles to select a style that will override any other formatting that has been applied to the cell.

9 Tap on this button to select a format for numbers in a cell

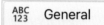

10 Tap on this button to select the properties for the selected number formatting option

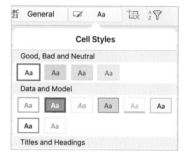

11 Tap on this button to select a style for the cell

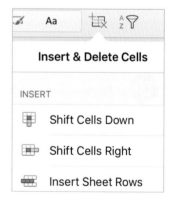

12 Tap on this button to insert or delete cells, rows and columns

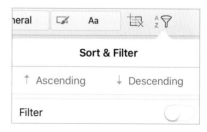

13 Tap on this button to sort and filter content in a column

Excel: Working with Tables

Within tables in Excel it is possible to format cells, rows and columns to your own design and size. To do this:

1 Tap on a letter at the top of a table to select a whole column

2 Drag here to expand the width of the column

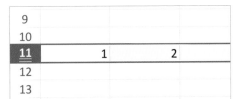

3 Tap on a number at the left-hand side of a table to select a whole row

4 Drag here to expand the height of the row

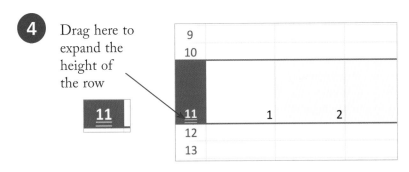

Don't forget

When a column is selected this also activates the column toolbar which can be used to cut and copy the column, insert a new column to the left of the selected one, clear the contents of the column, hide the column, or autofit the column to its contents (so it is just big enough for the content).

111

Hot tip

Press and hold on a cell to drag it into another position within the table.

...cont'd

5 Tap on a cell to select it

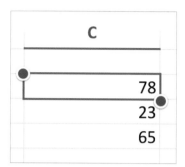

6 Drag these handles to expand the selection over a group of cells

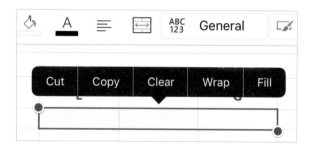

7 Select two or more cells that you wish to merge

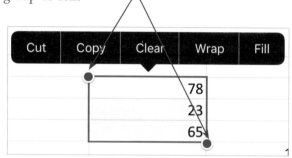

8 Tap on this button on the **Home** toolbar to merge the cells

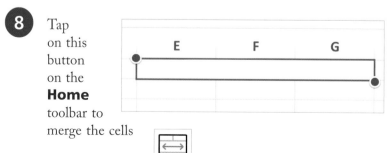

Excel: Creating Charts

Creating charts from data in a spreadsheet is an important way of displaying information in a more visually appealing format for work colleagues, either individually or in a presentation. To create and work with charts:

1 Select a range of cells as shown in Steps 5 and 6 on the previous page

2 Tap on the **Insert** tab on the Ribbon

Insert

3 Tap on the **Charts** button

 Charts

4 Select a style for the chart

5 Tap on one of the options for the style of the chart

Other items on the **Insert** tab on the Ribbon include: **Table**, **Pictures**, **Camera** (for taking a photo to include in a spreadsheet), **Shape** and **Text Box**.

The more cells of data that are selected, the greater the complexity of the chart that is created.

113

...cont'd

6 The chart is created using the data in Step 1

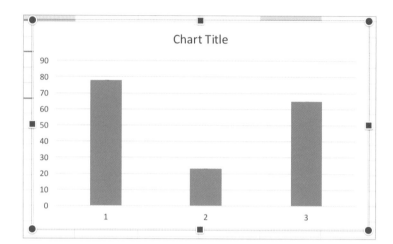

Don't forget

Tap on a chart to select it (and activate the **Chart** toolbar). Tap anywhere away from a chart to deselect it.

7 When a chart is created, or selected by tapping on it, the **Chart** toolbar is activated

Hot tip

The **Recommended** button on the **Chart** toolbar can be used to display suggested chart formats for the currently selected chart, based on the type and amount of data that has been selected for that chart.

8 Tap on the **Types** button to change the type of chart

9 Select a new type of chart, e.g. from columns to a pie chart

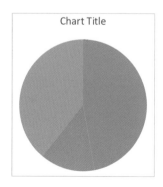

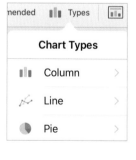

10 Tap on the **Layouts** button to change how the data in the chart is displayed

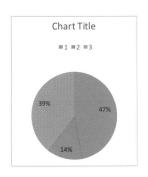

11 Tap on the **Elements** button to select how items within the chart are displayed, e.g. the **Chart Title**

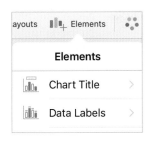

12 Tap on the **Colors** button to change the color scheme for the chart

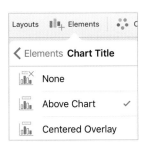

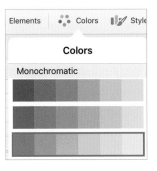

Hot tip

To change the Chart Title, double-tap on it within the chart to select it and then over-write the text as required.

115

Don't forget

The **Styles** button on the **Chart** toolbar can be used to apply an overall theme to a chart.

Excel: Formulas

Adding formulas to spreadsheets is what gives them a lot of their functionality, and changes them from just being a simple list of figures. Formulas can range from the relatively straightforward, to the complex and they are an essential feature of any spreadsheet that requires some form of calculation. To add formulas:

Hot tip

AutoSum can also be applied without first selecting any cells. To do this, tap on the **AutoSum** button and select the type of sum to perform. Then select the cells you want included in the sum.

1 Tap on the **Formulas** tab on the Ribbon

2 The most common type of formula is **AutoSum**, where the calculation is performed on selected cells. Select a range of cells

3 Tap on the **AutoSum** button

4 Select the type of calculation that you want to perform, e.g. **SUM**, which adds up all of the selected cells

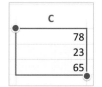

5 The result is displayed underneath the selected cells

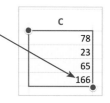

6 The cell contains the formula, not the figure displayed as the result. Tap on the cell containing the formula. This is displayed in the input box at the top of the window

Hot tip

Tap on the **fx** button to the left of the formula input field to view the most recently used functions. Formulas can also be created manually this way (see next page).

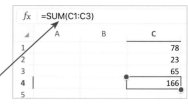

Creating formulas manually

As well as using AutoSum it is also possible to create your own formulas manually. To do this:

1 Tap on the **Formulas** tab and tap on the **fx** button to the left of the formula input field

2 The **=** symbol indicates that what follows is a formula

3 Tap on the numbers button above the keyboard

123

4 Tap on the **SUM** button

Σ

5 The **SUM** function is entered into the formula input field

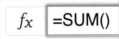

6 Create a formula by tapping on cells and

entering the required mathematical symbols to create the sum (the items within the brackets are calculated first and then the items outside the brackets are applied)

7 Press and hold on a key with a green tab in the corner to access additional symbols to use in the formula

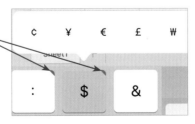

8 Tap on this button to apply the formula

Hot tip

If you move a cell containing a formula, the formula will move with it. If the content cells are moved together with the formula, the latter will update accordingly.

Don't forget

The other options for adding formulas on the Formulas toolbar are: **Recent**, **Financial Functions**, **Logical Functions**, **Text Functions**, **Date & Time Functions**, **Lookup & References Functions**, **Math & Trigonometry Functions** and **More Functions**, covering **Statistical**, **Engineering**, **Info** and **Database**.

Don't forget

The **fx** button also provides access to the full range of functions.

Google Sheets

This is Google's spreadsheet app, found in the same suite as Google Docs and Google Slides. It can be used to create spreadsheets and then store and share them online. To use Google Sheets:

1 Find **Google Sheets** in the **App Store** and tap on the **Get** button and then the **Install** button to download **Google Sheets**

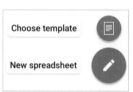

Google Sheets
Google, Inc.
★★★★☆ (24)   INSTALL

2 Tap on this icon to create a new spreadsheet

3 Tap on either the **Choose template** or **New spreadsheet** buttons

Choose template

New spreadsheet

4 For a spreadsheet based on a template, tap on a template style to create a spreadsheet with the selected formatting

Adding content

Once a spreadsheet has been created in Sheets, text and numerical content can be added. To do this:

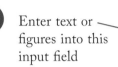 Tap on a cell in the spreadsheet

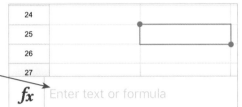

Enter text or figures into this input field

 Tap on this button to accept the content

 For text, tap on these button on the top toolbar to add bold, italics or strikethrough

B *I* ~~S~~

Tap on this button to select a **Text color** or a **Fill color** for the selected cell

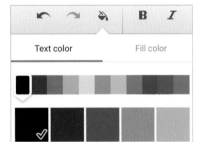

Tap on this button to add text formatting

Tap on the Back arrow at the top of a spreadsheet to go back to the main Sheets window.

 ← Monthly budget

119

Text formatting includes text font, text size and text color. It also has alignment options for text within cells.

...cont'd

Hot tip

To merge cells, tap on the first cell. Drag the selection handles over the required cells. Tap on the tab in Step 7 and next to **Merge cells** drag the button to the right so that it turns blue. Drag the button back again to split the merged cells.

Don't forget

To select a whole row in a spreadsheet, tap on one of the numbers in the left-hand column. To select a whole column, tap on one of the numbers on the top row. To expand a selected row or column, drag at the bottom or right of the number or letter respectively.

7 Tap on this tab to add cell formatting

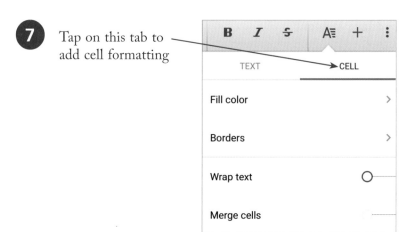

8 Tap on this button to insert items, including comments, new columns and rows

Adding formulas
To add formulas in Sheets:

1 Tap on the cell into which you want to insert the formula

2 To insert a formula manually, tap on the **=** symbol

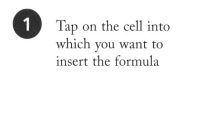

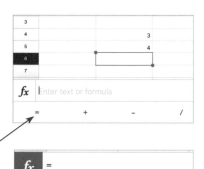

3 Tap on a cell to include it in the formula

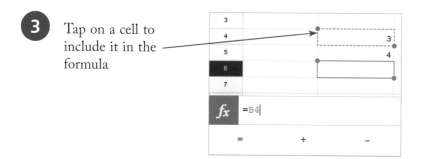

4 Tap on a mathematical symbol on the toolbar to include it in the formula

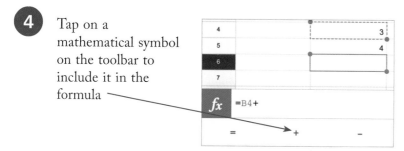

Don't forget

The cell labels, i.e. B4, B5, can also be inserted manually by typing, rather than selecting them within the spreadsheet.

5 Select other cells and symbols as required. Tap on this button to accept the formula

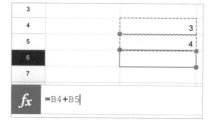

6 The target cell displays the result of the formula

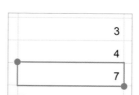

Don't forget

When a function is selected in Step 7, the data for the function then has to be included, to create the formula. This can be done manually, or by tapping on cells to select them.

7 Tap on the **fx** button to insert preset functions. The categories have additional options for specific functions

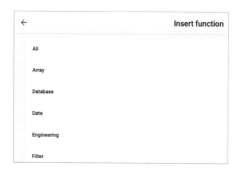

121

Spreadsheet Apps

The App Store has a range of spreadsheet apps, covering varying degrees of complexity. Some to try include:

iSpreadsheet Free

Combining simplicity of design with ease of use, but still powerful enough to create spreadsheets for the workplace that can also be opened in Excel and Pages. It is also compatible with iCloud, iCloud Drive and Google Drive.

OfficeSuite Pro

This is a paid-for suite of productivity apps that is designed to work with Microsoft Office documents. It contains powerful tools for creating spreadsheets, word processing documents and presentations. It can also be used to convert documents to PDF format.

Free Spreadsheet

Another free spreadsheet app, and one that has been designed to make creating and adding formulas as easy as possible. It supports a range of functions and also some options for creating graphs and charts. It can also import CSV files.

Polaris Office

Another productivity suite that includes a powerful spreadsheet app. There is a free version and also a paid-for version. It works primarily with Microsoft Office documents and also a number of cloud storage services including Dropbox, OneDrive and Amazon.

Spreadsheet Touch for Excel

This paid-for app is a version of Excel that has been designed specifically for use with touch on the iPad. It supports a wide range of functions for creating formulas and also charts and graphs.

CSV stands for Comma Separated Values and is used for numerical values and text. It is a format that is transferable between several different spreadsheet apps.

Complex spreadsheets, may lose some of their formatting if they are converted into CSV format and opened in another app.

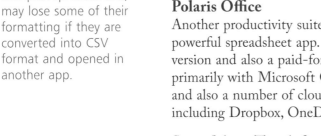

7 Presentations

It is hard to be in a business environment for any length of time without coming across a visual presentation at some point. This chapter looks at producing presentations with Apple's presentation app, Keynote, Microsoft PowerPoint, and Google Slides. For each app, there are details about creating presentations and adding text and graphical content. It also covers including transitions and builds in a presentation and showing it to an audience.

Keynote: Creating Presentations

Keynote is Apple's presentation app and it has been developed to a point where it is a realistic option for creating presentations in the workplace. The first step in Keynote is to create a new presentation. This can either be a blank template, or one from a template which includes pre-inserted content. To do this:

Don't forget

Keynote is not a built-in app, but it can be downloaded for free from the App Store.

1 Tap on the **Keynote** app

2 Tap on the **Create Presentation** button

3 Tap on one of the templates as the basis for the new presentation

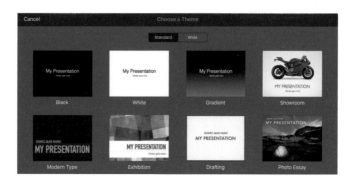

Don't forget

Once a presentation has been created it can have additional slides added to it.

4 Tap on content to select it and over-write it with your own content

Keynote: Saving Presentations

When a presentation is created in Keynote it is automatically saved within the Keynote file structure. From here it can be viewed and renamed. To do this:

1 From within the current presentation you are working on, tap on the **Presentations** button

2 The new presentation is displayed within the **Keynote** window

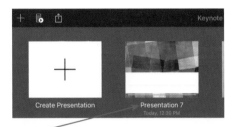

The thumbnail in the Keynote window displays the first slide of a presentation.

3 Tap on the presentation name to select it and access the **Rename Presentation** window

4 Enter a new name for the presentation

Beware

5 Tap on the **Done** button

6 Tap on the presentation, or any other in the **Keynote** window, to open it

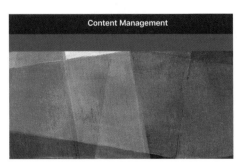

Use presentations sparingly, so that your audience does not become bored with them. They should be one in a range of methods for delivering information, not the only one.

Keynote: Adding Text

Text is one of the fundamental elements of a presentation (graphics being the other one). When a presentation is created from a template there are several pre-inserted text boxes. When subsequent slides are added they can be formatted with a variety of text box options.

Hot tip

Press and hold on a text box to drag it into a different position.

Hot tip

Double-tap on an individual word within a text box to format it separately from the other words in the text box. Tap on the button in Step 3, tap on the **Style** button and tap on the font name to format the selected word.

1 The title page of a presentation usually contains a main heading and subheading. Tap on a text box to select it and access its toolbar

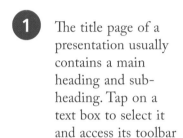

2 Double-tap on a text box and add your own text

3 With a text box selected (tap on it once), tap on this button on the top toolbar

4 Tap on the **Text** button

5 Make formatting selections for the text in the same way as for a Pages document (see page 58-60)

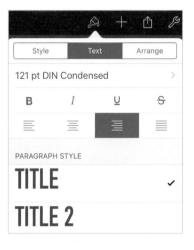

6 Tap on the **Style** button to apply a design style for the text box

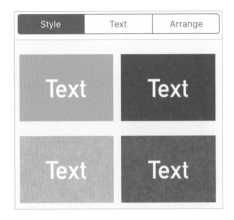

7 The style is applied to the whole text box

8 Tap on the **Arrange** button

Arrange

9 Drag this button to change the order of the text box within the slide

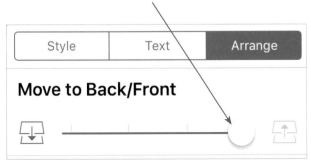

...cont'd

Don't forget

Text can be aligned to the top of a text box, the middle, or the bottom.

10 Tap on these buttons to specify text position within the text box

11 Tap on these buttons to specify a number of columns for the text box

1 Column — +

12 Tap on these buttons to specify the margin size for the text box

4 pt Margin — +

Text for new slides

When new slides are added to a presentation (see page 130) there are different options in terms of the types and numbers of text boxes that can be included:

Hot tip

Text can also be added by copying and pasting it from another app, such as Pages. This can be added to an existing text box, or a new one can be created by pasting the text into a blank area within a slide.

1 Tap on this button to add new slides to an existing presentation

2 Tap on one of the options for the new slide

Tap to add a slide.

LOREM IPSUM DOLOR

LOREM IPSUM DOLOR

LOREM IPSUM DOLOR

LOREM IPSUM

Beware

Do not use too much text in each slide of a Keynote presentation as it may have to be produced in a small font size in order to fit it on the slide, and this will make it difficult to read.

3 Double-tap on an item within a text box to add new text as required

DOUBLE-TAP TO EDIT

➤ Introduction

4 Tap on this button to format selected text

5 Tap on the **Style** button to format text within a text box

Style

Style | List | Layout

28 pt Iowan Old Style

B | *I* | U | S̶

PARAGRAPH STYLE

TITLE

The **Style** options for when text is selected are different to those when the whole text box is selected, as shown on page 127.

6 Tap on the **List** button to select formatting options for lists within a text box

List

Style | List | Layout

None

➤ Bullet

• Image

A. Lettered

7 Tap on the **Layout** button to select layout and positioning options for the selected text

Layout

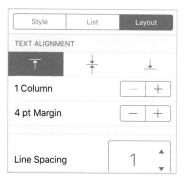

Style | List | Layout

TEXT ALIGNMENT

1 Column   − +

4 pt Margin   − +

Line Spacing   1

The **Layout** options for selected text are similar to those for a selected text box. For selected text, there is also a **Line Spacing** option.

Keynote: Adding Slides

The first slide of a presentation is usually an introductory one, which may have the subject and speaker's name. Subsequent slides can be added to the presentation, appropriate to the content that they will contain. Slides in a presentation can also be managed in the slides panel. To add new slides and work with them:

1 Tap on this button in the bottom left-hand corner of the screen

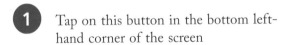

2 Swipe up and down to view the available slide formats

3 Tap on a slide format to add it as a new slide to the presentation

It is possible to add a completely blank new slide, with no content.

4 The slide is displayed in the main window, ready for new content to be added, and also as a thumbnail in the slides panel at the left-hand side

Swipe up and down in the slides panel to see all of the thumbnails of the slides in the presentation.

5 Different templates can be used for each new slide, or the same style can be used for the whole presentation

6 Press and hold on a thumbnail in the slides panel and drag it to change its position within the presentation

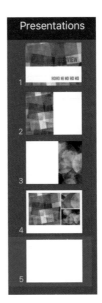

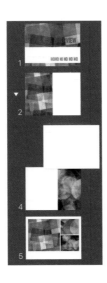

7 Tap on a slide in the slides panel to make it the active one

The toolbar in Step 8 also has an option to **Skip** the selected slide in the presentation and select a **Transition** for the slide and the next one (see pages 132-133).

8 Tap on an active slide in the slides panel and tap on these buttons to **Cut**, **Copy** or **Delete** the slide

Keynote: Transitions

When giving a presentation, moving between slides is done by tapping on the screen. The movement from one slide to another is known as a transition. By default, this contains no effect; the next slide simply appears. However, you can be more artistic and add a range of graphical transitions between slides. To do this:

1 Tap on a slide in the slides panel

2 Tap on this button on the top toolbar

3 Tap on the **Transitions and Builds** button

4 Tap on this button next to the slide thumbnail

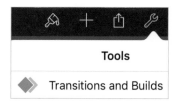

5 Tap on the required transition effect to add this to the slide (the effect will take place when the slide with the transition moves to the next one)

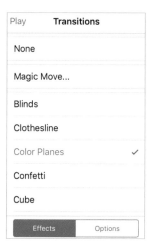

6 Tap on the **Options** button to select how the transition operates

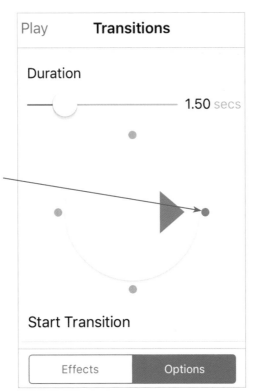

Play **Transitions**

Duration

1.50 secs

Start Transition

Effects | Options

7 Tap on the dots around the circle to set the direction of the transition effect

Do not set the **Duration** of the transition too fast, otherwise the effect may not be readily obvious.

8 Tap on the **Play** button to preview the transition

Play

9 Tap on the **Done** button to complete the transition

Done

10 When the **Transitions and Builds** button is selected, as in Step 3, tap on a slide thumbnail in the slides panel to view the type of transition that has been added

To delete a transition, tap on the transition name in Step 10 and select **None** for the type of transition.

Color Planes ›

Keynote: Adding Objects

Graphical items such as tables, objects, graphs and photos can be added to Keynote presentations in a similar way as for Pages and Numbers. To do this:

1 Tap on this button on the top toolbar

2 Tap on this button to add tables to the presentation

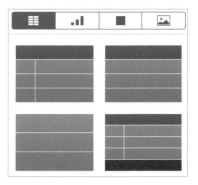

3 Tap on this button to add graphs and charts to the presentation

4 Tap on this button to add objects to the presentation

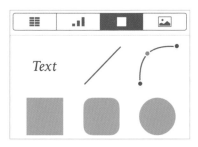

5 Tap on this button to add photos or videos to the presentation

Hot tip

Tap on the **Text** button in the objects window in Step 4 to add a new text box to a presentation.

Hot tip

Photos and videos can also be added by tapping on this button from within an existing graphical element.

6 Tap on an object to select it. Press and hold to drag the object into a new position

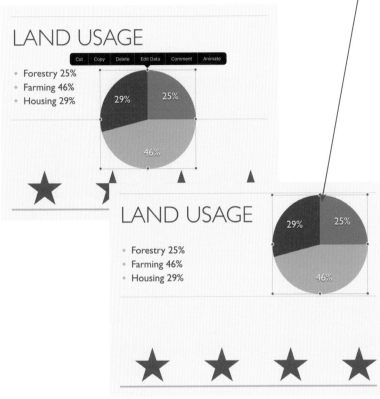

Tap once on tables, graphs, charts, objects or photos in a presentation to select them and access their relevant toolbar. This can then be used to perform tasks such as **Cut**, **Copy**, **Delete** and **Comment**.

7 Drag on these handles to resize an object

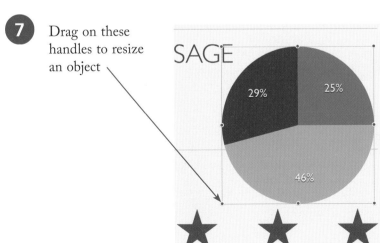

For a pie chart, tap on it once to select it. Press and hold on a wedge of the chart to drag it into a new position, detached from the rest of the chart.

Keynote: Builds

Most Keynote presentations consist of a number of items: text boxes, images, tables, graphs and objects. Each of these can be thought of as a separate entity and actions can be applied to each of them. This is known as "builds", and affects how each item appears on the slide. To add builds to a presentation:

Builds can be applied to several items of the same type of content, i.e. if you have five text boxes in a presentation, builds can be applied to all of them separately.

1 Select a slide that has a number of different types of content

As with transitions, do not use too many different build types within the same slide.

2 Tap on this button on the top toolbar

3 Tap on the **Transitions and Builds** button

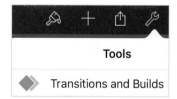

Each item can have a build in or a build out effect applied to it, or it can have both, e.g. it has a build in effect to appear in the slide and then a build out effect to remove it afterwards.

4 Tap on one of the content boxes to select it

5 Tap on either the **build in** or **build out** buttons

...cont'd

6 Select a build effect and tap on the **Play** button

7 Tap on the **Options** button at the bottom of the window to select how the build effect operates. This includes the speed of the build effect and the direction from where it appears (or disappears) on the slide)

Play	**Build In**	
None		
Anvil		
Appear		
Blinds		✓
Blur		
Comet		
Confetti		
Cube		
Effects	Options	Order

Build effects are activated in presentation mode. Each time you tap on the screen, one of the build effects will take place, e.g. tap once, a graphic will appear, tap again and a text box will appear, and so on.

8 Repeat the process to add build effects to the other items of content. Each item is numbered according to its position in the build sequence

137

Food science

Enhancing diet

The build out effect can be used to remove an item at the end of discussing a slide, before you move on to the next one. A build out effect is indicated by a gray box (a build in effect has a yellow box). It can be numbered to be activated at any point after the build in effect for the item.

9 Tap on the **Done** button   Done

Keynote: Presenter Notes

When a presentation is played to an audience, there is usually a presenter who delivers a narrative for the slides. This can be created separately from the Keynote presentation, or notes can be added to the slides themselves. To do this:

When giving a presentation, do not just read what is on the slides, word for word. The narrative should enhance the content of the slides: the content on the slides should display the main points, which are then developed in the narrative.

Don't forget

To print a slide with presenter notes, tap on the button in Step 1 and tap on the **Print** button. Select the layout with the thumbnail of the slide and the notes, and tap on the **Next** button. Select the required printer options and tap on the **Print** button.

1 Tap on this button on the top toolbar

2 Tap on the **Presenter Notes** button

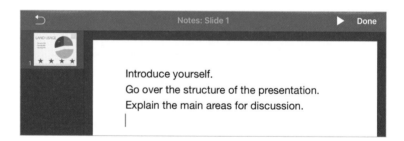

3 Notes can be added for each slide. Enter the required text and tap on the **Done** button

4 Notes can be printed out and used when giving the presentation (the notes are printed underneath a thumbnail of the slide to which they apply)

Keynote: Playing Presentations

The main purpose of creating a presentation is to be able to play it to an audience. This can be done via a projector onto a screen, or the iPad Pro could be used directly with its larger screen. When playing a presentation there are a number of tools that can be used by the presenter to aid the process. To play a presentation:

1 Tap on the first slide of the presentation in the slides panel

2 Tap on this button on the top toolbar

3 Tap on each slide to move forwards to the next one

OVERVIEW
NICK VANDOME

CONTENT MANAGEMENT
- What is Content Management?
- Do you need it?
- What does it do?
- What does it not do?
- Types of systems

4 Press and hold on a slide to access the presentation tools

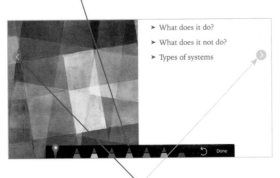

- What does it do?
- What does it not do?
- Types of systems

5 Tap on these buttons to move forwards or backwards in a presentation

Don't forget

The presentation starts playing at the slide that is selected in the slides panel in Step 1.

Hot tip

To exit presentation mode before the end of the presentation, pinch inwards with two fingers.

Don't forget

If transitions and builds have been added to a slide these will be activated each time you tap on a slide, until they have all been actioned.

Don't forget

A light pen (or laser pen) can also be used instead of the button in Step 6.

6 Tap on this button to highlight an item in a presentation (this operates in a similar way to using a light pen on a screen)

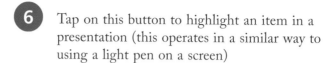

CONTENT MANAGEMENT

➤ What is Content Management?

140

Don't forget

When adding annotations to a slide, make sure you use a color that is a good contrast with any background on the slide.

7 Tap on these buttons to annotate items on screen

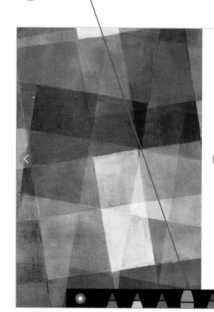

CONTENT MANAGEMENT

➤ What is Content Management?
➤ Do you need it?
➤ What does it do?
➤ What does it not do?
➤ Types of systems

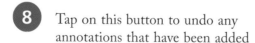

8 Tap on this button to undo any annotations that have been added

9 Tap on the **Done** button to exit the presentation tools

Keynote: Settings

Keynote has a range of settings for both creating and playing a presentation. To access these:

1 Tap on this button on the top toolbar to access the Keynote **Tools**

2 Tap on the **Presentation Tools** button

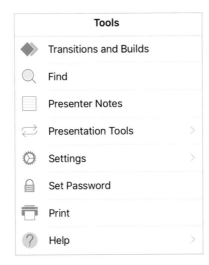

Tools	
◆	Transitions and Builds
○	Find
▭	Presenter Notes
⇄	Presentation Tools >
⚙	Settings >
🔒	Set Password
🖶	Print
?	Help >

3 Within Presentation Tools, there are options for adding Interactive Links, a Soundtrack, specifying the Presentation Type and using a Remote Control

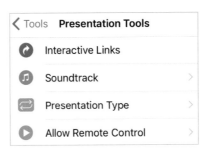

‹ Tools Presentation Tools	
↗	Interactive Links
♫	Soundtrack >
⇄	Presentation Type >
▶	Allow Remote Control >

4 Tap on the **Settings** button in Step 2 for the general Keynote settings, including options to Check Spelling, and adding Slide Numbers, Guides and Comments

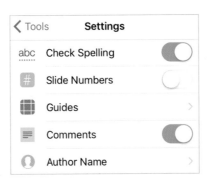

‹ Tools Settings	
abc	Check Spelling ⬤
#	Slide Numbers ○
⊞	Guides >
≡	Comments ⬤
◯	Author Name >

The Presentation Tools can also be used to **Find** a word or phrase in a presentation, **Set Password** to protect a presentation or **Print** it.

Interactive Links in Step 3 can be added to items in a slide to give them additional functionality, such as linking to other slides in the presentation, web pages or email links. This is a good way to increase navigational functionality within a presentation.

Presentation Type in Step 3 can be used to loop a presentation so that it keeps playing, i.e. it goes back to the first slide after it reaches the end, rather than going back to edit mode.

PowerPoint: Creating Files

Microsoft PowerPoint is part of the Office suite of productivity apps which can be downloaded and opened as shown on pages 37-39. Once this has been done, PowerPoint can be used to create presentations:

1 Tap on the **PowerPoint** app

2 Tap on the **New** button in the left-hand panel

3 Tap on one of the templates (including **Blank Presentation** to create a presentation with no content)

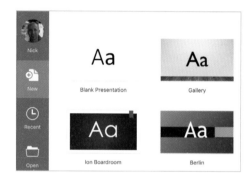

142

4 The presentation is created based on the selected template

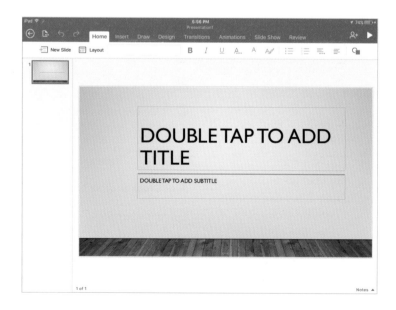

PowerPoint: Adding Content

Text is the main type of content that is added to PowerPoint slides, and there is also a range of other content that can be added to make them visually appealing.

1 Double-tap on a text box to add your own text

DOUBLE TAP TO ADD TITLE

DOUBLE TAP TO ADD SUBTITLE

2 Double-tap on text to select it

3 Tap on the **Home** button to access the text formatting tools

4 The text formatting tools are similar to those for Word (see pages 72-73). Use them to, from left to right, select layout, font and size, bold, italics, underlining, formatting, text color, WordArt style, bulleted and numbered lists and text alignment

5 Tap on the **Insert** tab to add tables, pictures, photos (from the iPad's camera), videos, shapes and text boxes

Limit the amount of text used in PowerPoint slides, otherwise it may become hard for the audience to take it in.

When text is selected, it also accesses the toolbar from which you can **Cut** or **Copy** the text, or tap on **Suggest** for an alternative to the word.

The **Insert** tab in PowerPoint is similar in operation to the one in Word (see pages 73-74 for details).

PowerPoint: Adding Slides

Presentations rarely consist of a single slide, and being able to add and format additional slides is an important part of PowerPoint.

Tap on the **Layout** button on the **Home** tab to select a new layout for an existing slide. The options are the same as for creating a new slide in Step 3.

Press and hold on a slide in the slide panel to drag it into a different position in the presentation.

Tap on the **Design** tab and select **Themes** to apply a theme to the whole presentation.

144

1. Tap on either the **Home** or the **Insert** tab at the top of the PowerPoint window

Home

Insert

2. Tap on the **New Slide** button

 New Slide

3. Select a style for the new slide

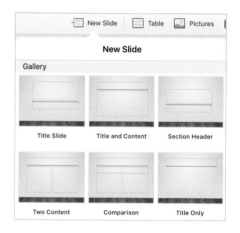

4. The slide is added to the presentation and also visible in the slide panel at the left-hand side

PowerPoint: Transitions

Once two or more slides have been created in a presentation, transitions can be applied to them. This determines the effect when one slide moves to another. To do this:

1 Tap on the **Transitions** tab

2 Tap on the **Transition Effect** button

3 Select one of the transition effects

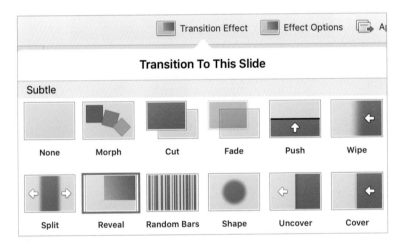

4 Tap on the **Effect Options** button to apply specific properties to the effect, such as coming in from the left or right, or vertically from the top or bottom

5 Tap on the **Apply To All** button to apply the selected effect to all of the slides in the presentation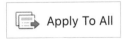

6 Tap on this button to play the presentation and view the transition effects between slides

Beware

Limit the number of different transitions within a presentation to two or three, otherwise it may become a bit bewildering for the audience.

Hot tip

Experiment with various transitions to see which ones you like best.

Don't forget

Slides to which transitions have been applied have a small star to the left of their icon in the slide panel.

Beware

The timings for transitions are preset and cannot be changed.

PowerPoint: Animations

As well as transitions, animations can be applied to specific items within a slide. This determines how they appear into a slide and exit from it. To add animated effects:

Don't forget

Items to which animations can be applied include text boxes, images, table, shapes and videos.

Don't forget

The **Entrance Effects** and **Exit Effects** have the same range of options, while those for **Emphasis Effects** vary slightly.

Hot tip

The **Emphasis Effect** is displayed by swiping on the slide once in Slide Show view. Tapping again moves on to the next effect.

1 Tap on the **Animations** tab

2 Tap on an item in a slide to select it

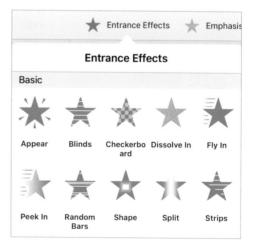

Customer Service

3 Tap on this button to give the item an entrance effect, i.e. how it first appears on the slide

 ⭐ Entrance Effects

⭐ Entrance Effects   ⭐ Emphasis

Entrance Effects

Basic

Appear | Blinds | Checkerbo ard | Dissolve In | Fly In

Peek In | Random Bars | Shape | Split | Strips

4 Tap on this button to give the item an emphasis effect

⭐ Emphasis Effects

5 Tap on this button to give the item an exit effect, i.e. how it leaves the slide before moving on to the next one

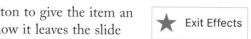 ⭐ Exit Effects

PowerPoint: Slide Shows

Once the slides of a presentation have been completed it can be shown to an audience as a slide show. To do this:

1 Tap on this button to **Play** the presentation as a slide show

2 Swipe on a slide to move to the next one (or activate any animations that have been applied)

3 Tap at the top of the screen to access the top toolbar

4 Tap on this button to use a pen to draw on the slide

5 Tap on this button to select settings for the pen, including color, size and an eraser option for removing pen marks

6 Tap on this button to hide the current slide and show a black screen. Tap on the button again to reveal the slide

7 Tap on this button to minimize the current presentation so that presenter notes can be added to the slides

8 Tap on this button to exit the presentation

Don't forget

Swipe to the left to show the next slide; swipe to the right to show the previous slide.

Hot tip

Tap on the **Slide Show** tab to access options to play the presentation **From Start** or **From Current** slide. You can also access **Presenter View**, from where you can add presenter notes to the slides, and tap on **Hide Slide** to hide a slide in a presentation.

Don't forget

As with Word and Excel, tap on this button on the top toolbar to access **Sharing** options for the current presentation. See page 79 for details.

Google Slides

This is Google's presentation app in the same suite as Google Docs and Google Sheets. It can be used to create presentations and then store and share them online. To use Google Slides:

As with Google Docs and Google Sheets, you need a Google Account in order to use Google Slides, as shown on page 40.

1 Find **Google Slides** in the **App Store** and tap on the **Get** button and then the **Install** button to download **Google Slides**

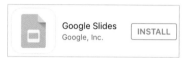

2 Tap on this icon to create a new presentation

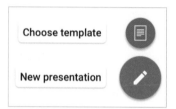

3 Tap on either the **Choose template** or **New presentation** buttons

You have to sign in with your Google Account details to use Google Slides. However, if you are already signed in to another Google productivity app (Docs or Sheets) you will be able to continue using Slides without signing in again.

4 For a presentation based on a template, tap on a template style to create a presentation with the selected formatting

5 The presentation is created, based on the template in the previous step

Presentations based on a template already have a number of slides pre-inserted, not just the introductory slide. These appear in the left-hand slide panel. Press and hold on a thumbnail in the slide panel to drag it into a different position in the presentation.

6 If you select **New presentation** in Step 3, give it a name and tap on the **Create** button

149

Tap on this button to go back to the main Google Slides window, in the same way as for Google Docs as shown on page 82.

7 The presentation is created in the Google Slides window. Tap on this button to save editing changes to a presentation

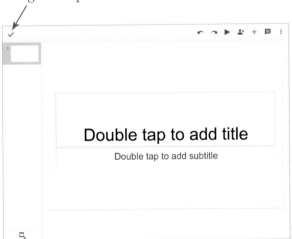

...cont'd

Working with slides

Once a new presentation has been created, content can be added to slides. The slides themselves can also be managed and played within the presentation:

Beware

There are no transitions effects or animations available in Google Slides.

1 Double-tap on a text box to add your own content

Don't forget

The text formatting options include selecting font, font size, text color and highlight color.

2 Double-tap on a word to select it and use these buttons to add bold, italics or underlining

3 Tap on this button to select text formatting options

Don't forget

The paragraph formatting options include text alignment (left, middle, right and justify), text position (top, middle or bottom), indent and outdent, numbered and bulleted lists and line spacing.

4 Tap on the **Paragraph** tab to select paragraph formatting options

5 Tap on this button to add additional content including text boxes, images and shapes

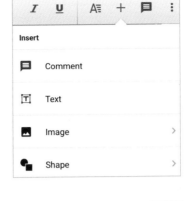

Tap on this button to access the presentation's menu.

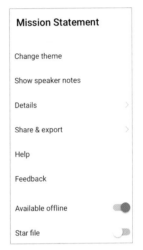

6 Tap on this button at the bottom of the slide panel to add a new slide to the presentation

151

7 Tap on this button to **Share** the presentation

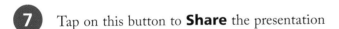

Tap on this button to **Play** the presentation, either to review the content or for an audience. Swipe to the left to move to the next slide (or tap on the screen); swipe to the right to move to the previous one. There are no annotation tools in Play mode.

8 Enter the email addresses for anyone with whom you want to share the presentation, and tap on this button. Tap on this button to access the Share menu to specify who has access to the presentation

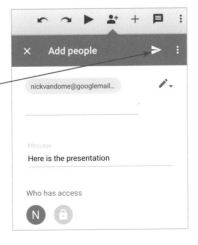

Presentation Apps

The App Store has a range of presentation apps, covering different levels of sophistication. Some to try include:

Prezi Lite Editor

A free presentation app that has been designed with workers on the move, such as sales staff, firmly in mind. Presentations can be created from scratch and shared via email or any chat app. They can also be displayed on a television, using Apple TV's AirPlay.

SlideShark

An elegant presentation tool that can be used to share PowerPoint presentations. They are uploaded from your iPad to a free, secure cloud account. It can also be used to download presentations, and it integrates with other cloud services such as Dropbox.

AstralPad Office Collaboration

This is a productivity suite of apps that can be used with Microsoft Office documents. It includes a presentation app, and content can be presented to clients remotely. It is also collaborative and you can invite colleagues to view documents and edit them.

Haiku Deck

One of the most attractive presentation apps that specializes in elegant charts and graphs. There is also a range of graphical themes that can be used as the foundation of a presentation, and they can be shared via the web or on your own business website.

Presentation Clock

One of the several presentation clock apps that are in the App Store. These can be used to set up timings for your presentations. Several timers can be set up and saved, and the timer changes color as different time limits are reached. Timers can also be used to give audible or vibration alerts.

Don't forget

Presentation apps such as SlideShark and AstralPad Office are cloud-based so require a fast internet connection to edit and present documents.

Hot tip

Cloud-based presentation tools require you to sign in or register, before you can start using them.

8 Organization Apps

In a busy working environment, it is important to keep as organized as possible. This chapter looks at some apps to help you achieve this.

Using the Notes App

Notes is the built-in note-taking app on the iPad. It is ideal for jotting down work ideas, agendas for meetings, or an outline for a talk or presentation. Content such as photos can also be added within the Notes app and there is a facility to add handwritten content. To use the Notes app:

Don't forget

Set up iCloud for Notes (**Settings > iCloud** and drag the **Notes** button to **On**) so that your notes will be stored here and be available on any other iCloud-enabled devices that you have.

1 Tap on the **Notes** app

2 Tap on this button to create a new note. This activates the virtual keyboard, or the Shortcuts bar with the Smart Keyboard

3 As the note is created, it appears in the left-hand Notes panel. The most recent note is at the top and the first line of the note is the title. Tap on a note to view and edit it

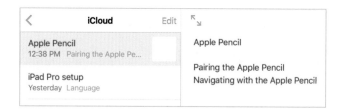

Hot tip

Content can be shared to Notes from apps such as Safari, Maps and Photos. This creates a note with a link to the appropriate app. To do this, tap on the **Share** button in an appropriate app and select Notes.

4 Tap on this button to delete the current note

5 Tap on this button to share a note, copy, lock or print it

Don't forget

Notes can be shared to Messages, Mail, Facebook and Twitter.

...cont'd

Formatting notes

To apply formatting to text in a note:

1 Double-tap on a word to select it and access its toolbar

2 Drag the yellow handles over selected additional text as required

Pairing the Apple Pencil
Navigating with the Apple Pencil

3 Tap on this button to access the formatting options

4 Tap on one of the formatting options, such as Title, Heading or Body for formatting the font and size, or the list options for creating a list from the selection

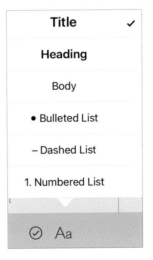

Title ✓

Heading

Body

• Bulleted List

– Dashed List

1. Numbered List

⊘ Aa

5 The formatting is applied to the selected text (a **Title**, in this instance)

Apple Pencil

Pairing the Apple Pencil
Navigating with the Apple Pencil

Items can be selected in Notes by double-tapping with either your finger or the Apple Pencil.

When text is selected, the toolbar that appears can be used to **Cut** or **Copy** the text, **Paste** text that has already been copied, **Replace** the selected text, apply **Bold**, **Italics** or **Underlining**, show a dictionary definition or **Share** the text.

The range of text styles is fairly limited in Notes and additional styles cannot be added.

...cont'd

6 Select one or more lines of text

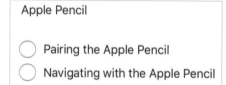

7 Tap on this button to create a checklist from the selected text

8 Radio buttons are added to the list (these are the round buttons to the left-hand side of the text)

9 Tap on the radio buttons to show that an item or a task has been completed

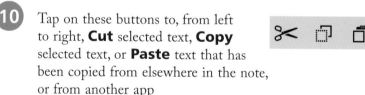

10 Tap on these buttons to, from left to right, **Cut** selected text, **Copy** selected text, or **Paste** text that has been copied from elsewhere in the note, or from another app

11 Tap on this button to add a photo or a video to the note (either by taking one, or from your Photo Library on your iPad)

12 Tap on this button to add a freehand sketch or note

Don't forget

On the iPad Pro with the Smart Keyboard connected, tap on this button to hide the Shortcuts bar.

Don't forget

On the iPad using the virtual keyboard, tap on this button to hide the keyboard and also the Shortcuts bar.

13 Select a pen style and color at the bottom of the screen and draw on the screen to create freehand content

A good option for creating freehand content in Notes is with the Apple Pencil on the iPad Pro. However, you can also use your finger.

14 Tap on these buttons to, from left to right, finish a drawing and return to Notes, undo the previous action, redo the previous undo action and remove all content

15 The freehand content is added to the current note

When a sketch is added to a note, a thumbnail of it is included next to the note in the Notes panel.

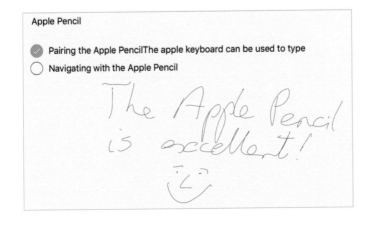

Notability

Notability is one of the most popular notes apps in the App Store and it offers an attractive interface and a range of powerful features for effective note-taking. Some of its features include:

- It has been optimized for use with the Apple Pencil so you can create handwritten notes in this way. There is also a **Stop using Apple Pencil** button so that you can write with your finger if required.

- There is a wide selection of pencil thicknesses.

- There is a wide selection of paper types that can be selected from the Utilities button (spanner icon). These include colored papers, lined and squared.

- There is a highlighter that can be used to highlight typed or handwritten text.

- Notes can be created as more than one page and these are displayed as thumbnails in the sidebar.

- Voice recordings can be attached to notes.

- Notes are automatically saved as you type or write.

To use Notability:

Hot tip

It is easier to write notes with the Apple Pencil when the iPad Pro is lying flat, rather than upright with the Smart Keyboard attached.

Don't forget

When using the Apple Pencil, the touchscreen function is disabled, so you can rest your hand on the screen while writing, without activating anything.

Don't forget

Create **Subjects** and **Dividers** to keep your notes as organized as possible.

1 Download **Notability** from the App Store and tap on this icon to open it

2 Tap on this button to create a new **Subject**, which holds notes, or a **Divider**, which groups subjects

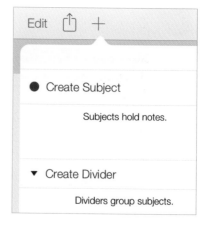

3 Tap on a **Subject** into which you want to create a new note and tap on this button

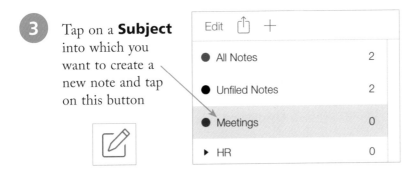

4 Use these buttons to, from left to right, add typewritten **Text** (this also activates the text Shortcuts bar above the keyboard), select **Pencil** type and color, select **Highlighter**, select **Eraser**, select **Scissors** to select items to cut, copy or paste, and **Move** around a note

5 Use these buttons to, from left to right, add a **Voice Recording** to a note, add **Media** including photos and shapes, add **Utilities** such as paper type and view the **Pages Sidebar**

6 Tap on this button to **Share** notes via email, Twitter, Facebook, or any online cloud services to which you are subscribed

Destination

✉ Email

✲ Dropbox

▲ Google Drive

🐦 Twitter

The Eraser function deletes the latest complete action in its entirety, i.e. if you have written a word in one action the Eraser will remove the whole word, rather than just being able to remove part of it.

The **Pencil** option in Step 4 also contains the **Stop using Apple Pencil** button.

Tap on this button to **Import** notes from an online cloud service to which you are subscribed.

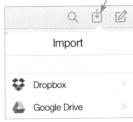
Import

✲ Dropbox

▲ Google Drive

OneNote

This is the note-taking app from Microsoft that can be downloaded individually, and is also included in the Microsoft Office suite of apps. To use OneNote:

1 Download **OneNote** from the App Store and tap on this icon to open it

2 Notes are stored in the left-hand notes sidebar. Tap on the tabs at the top to view notes in different categories. Tap on this button to create a new tab

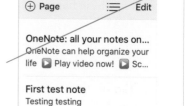

3 Tap on this button to create a new note

4 Use the Ribbon tabs (**Home**, **Insert**, **Draw** and **View**) to format text and add content to your notes (this is similar to using the Ribbon in Word, see pages 72-78 for details)

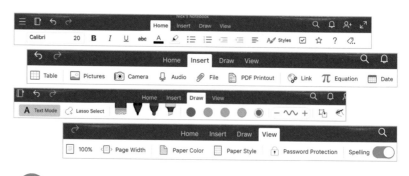

160

5 Enter a title for the note and body text. The box for the body text can be moved by dragging here

Calendar

The built-in Calendar app on the iPad can be used to organize your appointments and meetings:

1 Tap on the **Calendar** app

2 Tap here to view the calendar by Day, Week, Month or Year view. Swipe up or down to move between days, weeks, months or years

Day	Week	Month	Year

3 Tap on the **Today** button to view the current date

Today

4 Tap on this button to create a new event, or press and hold on a selected date to add an event there

+

5 Enter a **Title** and a **Location** for the event

Cancel	New Event	Add
Team Builiding		
Conference Room		⊗

6 Drag the **All-day** button from **On** to **Off** and tap on **Starts** and **Ends** to set these details

All-day		
Starts	May 13, 2016	11:00 AM
Ends		2:00 PM

7 Select **Repeat** for a recurring event, **Invitees** to invite people to an event, or **Alert** to set an alert before the event. Finally, tap on **Add** at the top of the window to create the event in the calendar

Repeat	Never >
Travel Time	None >
Calendar	● Work >
Invitees	None >
Alert	1 hour before >
Second Alert	None >
Show As	Busy >

If you work in an office environment you will probably have your own internal email and calendar facility. You may be able to connect to this through a VPN (Virtual Private Network) connection from **Settings > General > VPN > Add VPN Configuration**. Check with your IT Administrator first to check that this is allowed by your organization, and also to get the required VPN settings.

Microsoft Exchange is an email client that is widely used in the workplace. An iPad can be connected to an Exchange network from **Settings > Mail, Contacts, Calendars > Add Account > Exchange**.

Contacts

The built-in Contacts app on the iPad can be used to add contacts to your address book:

Beware

Groups of contacts can be created on a Mac computer using OS X and accessed in the Contacts app, by tapping on the **Groups** button (and in the Mail app by entering the group name in the **To** field of an email). However, groups cannot be created in Contacts on the iPad.

Hot tip

Tap on a green **+** button in the new contact window to add an extra field for that item. Tap on a red **-** button and tap on the **Delete** button to delete an item.

Hot tip

If a contact has **FaceTime** (Apple's video chatting app) then you will be able to make a FaceTime call directly from their entry in the Contacts app.

1. Tap on the **Contacts** app

2. Tap on this button to add a new contact

3. Enter the required details for a contact, including name, business name, phone number, email address, website address, messaging service and birthday

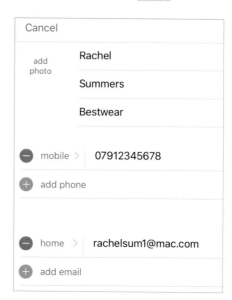

Cancel	
add photo	Rachel
	Summers
	Bestwear
⊖ mobile >	07912345678
⊕ add phone	
⊖ home >	rachelsum1@mac.com
⊕ add email	

4. Tap on the **Done** button
   Done

5. Use these buttons to contact someone via text message (iMessage) or share their contact details
   Send Message
   Share Contact

6. Tap on the **Edit** button to edit details for an individual entry
   Edit

7. To delete a contact, swipe to the bottom of the Edit window and tap on the **Delete Contact** button
   Delete Contact

Reminders

To ensure that you never miss another meeting or appointment, the Reminders app can be used to display alerts for specific events.

1 Tap on the **Reminders** app

2 The Reminder lists are located in the left-hand panel. Tap on the **New List** button for a list, or **Reminders** to create a new reminder

3 Tap on a new line and enter the reminder

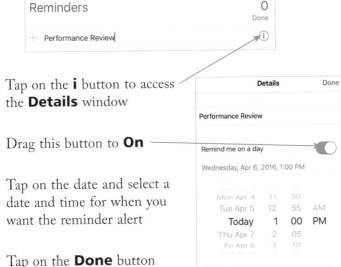

4 Tap on the **i** button to access the **Details** window

5 Drag this button to **On**

6 Tap on the date and select a date and time for when you want the reminder alert

7 Tap on the **Done** button

Done

8 At the date and time of the reminder, a pop-up box appears. Tap on **Mark as Completed** to close the reminder

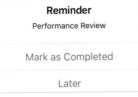

Set the date and time for reminders by dragging up and down on the relevant barrels within the **Details** window. The time can be set in five-minute intervals.

For a recurring reminder, tap on the **Repeat** link in the **Details** window (if **Remind me on a day** is **On**) and select a repeat option from Never, Every Day, Every Week, Every 2 Weeks, Every Month or Every Year. The reminder will then appear at the specified timescale, at the time set in Step 6.

Tap on the **Later** button in Step 8 and select a time for when you want the reminder to reappear.

Time Management Apps

There are several apps in the Productivity category of the App Store that can be used for time management tasks. Some to look at include:

Some time management apps require you to register for their cloud services and log in when using the app, even for some of the free ones.

164

Do

This free app can be used to organize and run meetings in the workplace. It can be used to schedule meetings, email details to the participants, create and share meeting agendas, make your own notes to be used in a meeting, or take notes during a meeting.

Wunderlist

This is a to-do list and task manager app for keeping up-to-date with what you need to do on a daily, weekly or monthly basis. It can be used to set due dates and reminders for important events, create and share lists, and add notes, files and comments to lists.

Due

Another app that can be used to remind you of events and meetings. Once an event has been entered, it keeps reminding you until an action is taken for the reminder. It also contains a countdown timer, and reminders can be entered with text or voice.

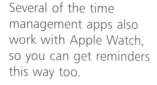

Several of the time management apps also work with Apple Watch, so you can get reminders this way too.

2Do

This is a powerful, paid-for time management app that not only enables you to create to-do lists, reminders and projects, but also lets you share and sync them with a large number of cloud services. It is an excellent option for linking tasks in the workplace.

Pocket Informant

This free app acts as a calendar, a task manager and a note-taker. It supports voice dictation and items can be synced to services such as Google Calendar and Evernote.

9

Sharing and Collaboration

This chapter looks at options for sharing documents with colleagues, and enabling them to view and edit them.

Sharing on the iPad

Considering the number of different computer operating systems that are in use (Windows, Mac OS X, iOS and Android to name a few) it is important to be able to share documents between these systems if you are using your iPad in the workplace. This can be done primarily through the different cloud services. Therefore, it is important that users of different systems have access to other cloud services as well as the one linked to their device.

Sharing with iCloud

Items stored in iCloud can be shared with other users by sending them a link to a document. You can also access your own iCloud documents through the iCloud app on a Windows PC, which can be downloaded from the iCloud page on the Apple website.

Sharing with Windows

Sharing documents that have been created in Windows is best done through Microsoft's OneDrive cloud service. In this way, documents that are created on a Windows PC can be shared on an iPad. This can be done through a browser or by downloading the OneDrive app onto your iPad (see page 170 for details).

Sharing with Android

Fewer documents will probably be created on Android devices for sharing in the workplace, but for those that are, the Google Drive is a good option (see page 169 for details). They can also be shared in Dropbox, from where other users will be able to access them (see page 168 for details).

General sharing

Sharing documents from the iPad can be done through the **Share** button.

Apps such as Pages, Numbers and Keynote also have an option for sharing documents online through iCloud, by sending a link to the recipient, who can then use it to access your document through a browser (see pages 66-67 for details).

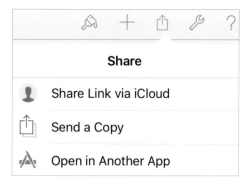

To have effective sharing and collaboration on your iPad, you should have access to different cloud sharing services and ensure other users have access to yours too.

Dropbox can be used to share documents from any device, not just Android ones.

Sharing with iCloud Drive

iCloud and iCloud Drive are most effective at storing your own documents and making them available to you on other devices. However, iCloud Drive can still be used to share documents with other people. To do this:

1 Tap on this app to open **iCloud Drive**

2 Tap on a folder to view the documents within it

3 Press and hold on the document to be shared and tap on the **More...** button

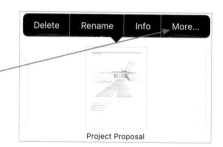

4 Tap on the **Share Item...** button

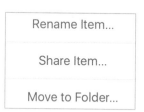

5 Select an option for sharing the item. If you have added other cloud service's apps to your iPad these will be available here

Hot tip

It is possible to access iCloud Drive files on a Windows PC by downloading the Windows version of iCloud from the Support section of the Apple website. This can then be used to access your iCloud documents and files when you are not using your iPad.

Beware

If you share an iCloud Drive document with someone via Google Drive, Dropbox or OneNote, check that they have a compatible app for opening it.

Sharing with Dropbox

Dropbox is a good option for sharing, as there are versions for most types of operating systems. This means that you can access your own documents in Dropbox from a variety of devices, and also give other people access to your documents by allowing them access to your folders. To do this:

1 Access your Dropbox account on your iPad (either by using the **Dropbox** app or by logging into your account at **www.dropbox.com** in Safari)

2 Tap here next to a folder to view its menu

3 Tap on the **Invite People to Collaborate** button

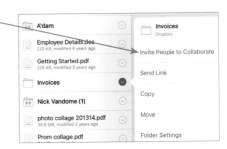

4 Tap under **Folder Permissions** to determine who can manage the folder

5 Select the required permissions for who can manage the folder and tap on the **Invite to Folder** back button

6 Tap on the **Invite** button to send an email invitation to the recipient

Sharing with Google Drive

Google Drive is a good option for sharing documents, including those created on an Android device and those created with the Google suite of apps: Google Docs, Google Sheets and Google Slides. To share items with Google Drive on your iPad:

 Download the Google Drive app from the App Store and tap on the **Google Drive** icon

2 Documents are stored in the **My Drive** section

3 Tap here next to an item to access its menu

4 Tap on the **Add people** button to invite work colleagues to view a document

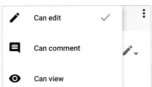

5 Enter the email addresses of people you want to share the document with

6 Tap here to specify what the recipient(s) can do with the document (edit, comment or just view)

7 Tap on the **Send** button. The recipient(s) will receive an email inviting them to view and edit the document online (without having to log in)

169

Don't forget

You must have a Google Account to sign in to the Google Drive app. This can be created with a username and password when you first open the app.

Hot tip

Tap on the **Send a copy** button in Step 4 to email a copy of the document.

Don't forget

Other people can share their documents in Google Drive with you, using the same process as shown here. To view your shared documents, tap on the top left-hand menu button and tap on the **Shared with me** button.

Sharing with OneDrive

OneDrive is the Microsoft cloud storage and sharing service, where items can be shared in a similar way to iCloud, Dropbox and Google Drive. To do this from your iPad:

Don't forget

You must have a Microsoft Account to sign in to the OneDrive app. This can be created with a username and password when you first open the app.

Don't forget

If you have a OneDrive folder on a Windows PC, its contents will automatically be visible in the OneDrive app on your iPad (as long as both of them are linked to the same Microsoft Account).

Hot tip

Documents can also be shared in OneDrive by copying the link and pasting it into an email, sending a link in an Outlook email or attaching the document to an email.

1 Download the OneDrive app from the App Store and tap on the **OneDrive** icon

2 Tap on the **Files** button

3 Tap on a folder to view the documents within it (these can have been added to OneDrive on a Windows PC)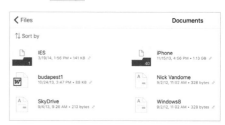

4 Press and hold on a file to select it

5 Tap on this button on the bottom toolbar

6 Tap on the **Invite People** button

7 Enter a recipient's email address or tap here to select them from your contacts

8 Tap on the **Add** button. The recipient(s) will receive an email inviting them to view and edit the document online (without having to log in)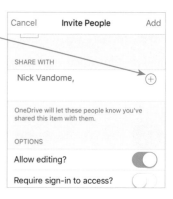

10 Email Management

It is easy to get swamped by email in the workplace and allow it to take over your working day. This chapter looks at how you can manage your email so that you stay in control of it.

About Email Management

Email in the workplace is a topic that can provoke strong opinions: some people think that it is an effective form of communication that they cannot do without; while others think it is the scourge of the modern workplace, leading to thousands of unnecessary messages and a loss of face-to-face contact. The truth is probably somewhere in between, but an undeniable fact is that email has to be managed effectively in the workplace, in order to get the best benefits from it.

Individual email management

Everyone in the workplace has responsibility for the email which they send and receive, and there are some steps that should be followed when using email:

- Ask yourself if you really need to send a particular email. Are you doing it through habit and is there a better way to communicate your message, such as face-to-face?

- Create folders for email covering different topics so that your Inbox does not become overflowing and hard to manage.

- Do regular housekeeping on your emails: delete the ones that are not needed and place the rest into folders.

- Avoid getting into arguments with colleagues in email conversations: it can be hard to gauge tone and nuance in an email and minor disagreements can quickly escalate.

- Never open attachments from people you don't know, even though they should have been scanned by your IT section before they reach you.

Corporate email management

Every organization that provides an email service for its employees should have the following in place:

- An Email Policy, covering what is allowed and what is not.

- Email Guidelines, which offer advice about using email effectively in the workplace.

- A robust system for backing up all corporate emails.

- A robust security system for scanning all emails that come into the organization before they reach their recipient.

Be careful when using **Reply All** to a group email. Ask yourself if everyone in the group needs to see your reply, or just the original sender of the message.

Never send inappropriate material on your corporate email network, even if you think you are just being humorous. If in doubt, don't send it.

Emails always leave an electronic footprint, even if they are deleted by the recipient. Think twice before sending an email that is critical of a colleague or your organization.

Email on the iPad

The default email app on the iPad is Mail. This can be used with an iCloud email account or linked to other email services. To add different email accounts:

1 Tap on the **Settings** app and tap on the **Mail, Contacts, Calendars** tab

2 Tap on the **Add Account** button

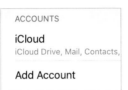

3 Select the type of account you want to add, including those for Exchange and Outlook

4 Enter your login details for the selected account (this has to be one that you are already registered for)

5 Once an email account has been added, it is included under the **Accounts** heading in the **Mail, Contacts, Calendars** tab of the **Settings** app

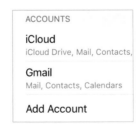

6 Open the **Mail** app and tap on the **Mailboxes** button. You can view the **Inboxes** from all of the linked email services, or just those from individual ones

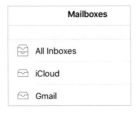

When you create an iCloud account with an Apple ID (username and password) an email account is automatically created for you.

Several email accounts can be added through the **Add Account** option in Steps 2 and 3 and emails from all of them can be displayed in the Mail app.

Email accounts can be deleted by tapping on them in Step 5 and tapping on the **Delete Account** button. However, this does not remove the content from the email server, and the account and its contents can be added again.

Creating Mailboxes

One of the most effective ways to organize your emails is through the use of mailboxes, so that you can sort them according to subject. To do this with Mail (the process is similar for other email apps):

One of the best ways to organize your Inbox is to delete emails that you no longer need.

To delete a mailbox, tap on it in Step 3 and tap on the **Delete Mailbox** button.

174

The mailboxes that are included by default cannot be deleted.

The **Done** button is at the top of the Mailbox panel and is available after the Save button has been tapped in Step 6.

1 Tap on the **Mail** app

2 The app should open at the **Inbox**. Tap on the **Mailboxes** button to view all of your mailboxes

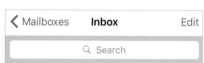

3 Some mailboxes are created in the app by default, e.g. **Drafts**, **Sent**, **Junk**

4 Tap on the **Edit** button at the top of the panel

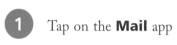

5 Tap on the **New Mailbox** button at the bottom of the panel

New Mailbox

6 Give the new mailbox a name and tap on the **Save** button

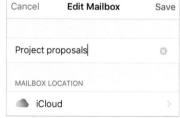

7 Tap on the **Done** button

Done

8 The new mailbox is added to the list in the Mailboxes panel

Managing Mailboxes

Although there are not as many options for managing emails on the iPad as for a desktop computer or laptop, there are still a number of ways in which you can work with them:

Moving emails

To move emails into mailboxes:

1 Tap on the **Edit** button in the Inbox panel

2 Tap next to an email to select it

3 Tap on the **Move** button at the bottom of the panel

4 Tap the mailbox into which you want to move the email

Adding mailbox shortcuts

Shortcuts can be added to, or removed from the Mailboxes panel:

1 Tap on the **Edit** button in the Mailboxes panel

2 Tap on items to add or remove them as a shortcut from the Mailboxes list

3 Tap on the **Add Mailbox** button to add one of your own mailboxes as a shortcut

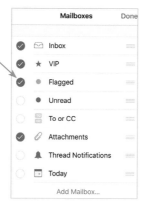

An email can also be moved by tapping on this button on the top toolbar in Mail and then selecting the required folder.

Next to the **Move** button in Step 3 are options to **Mark** or **Trash** a selected item. The **Mark** options are **Flag**, **Mark as Unread** and **Move to Junk**.

If you add an item as a shortcut in the Mailboxes panel, you will be able to view just these related items by tapping on it, e.g. to view all of your emails with attachments.

Using Flags

When you are dealing with a large number of emails, it can be useful to color-code them so that you have a visual guide to quickly identify emails from particular people, or on certain subjects. This can be done through the use of colored flags or symbols (also called labels in some email apps). However, only one type of flag can be applied, so you can only flag up one item at a time.

Beware

Different items can be flagged, but the currently flagged items have to be unflagged first (see Step 3).

Don't forget

To change the style of a flag, select **Settings > Mail, Contacts, Calendars > Flag style** and select either **Color** or **Shape**.

Hot tip

Flagged items can also be viewed by typing **Flags** into the **Inbox Search** box and tapping on the **Message is Flagged** button.

1 In the Mail app, enter a criteria in the **Inbox Search** box (this could either be a person's name or a subject)

2 Tap on the items you want to select and tap on the **Mark** button

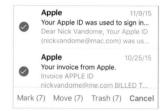

3 Tap on the **Flag** button (if the marked items are already flagged then the button will display **Unflag**)

4 The flag is applied to the selected item

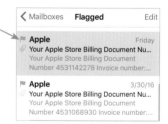

5 In the Mailboxes panel, tap on the **Flagged** mailbox to view all of the flagged items

Auto-Swipe

Since the iPad is designed for use with touch, it is logical that some of the functionality in the Mail app can be accessed through swiping, known as auto-swipe. To use this:

1 Tap on the **Settings** app and select **Mail, Contacts, Calendars > Swipe Options**

Swipe Options

2 Tap on the options for swiping left or right on an email

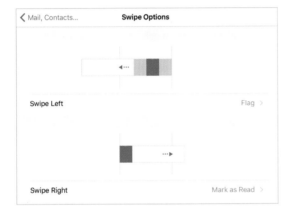

3 Select an action for each option

4 In the Mail app, access the Inbox and swipe left or right to apply the actions specified in the Swipe Options settings (see page 178)

The swipe options for both left and right can be set to **None**, if required.

The same action cannot be applied to swiping from both left and right, apart from **None**.

Swipe Actions

From within the Swipe Options (see Step 4 on the previous page, page 177) there are different actions that can be applied to individual messages:

(1) Tap on the **Trash** button to move the email to the Trash mailbox

Hot tip

If you swipe halfway across the width of the Inbox, the swipe option button appears. If you swipe the whole way across the default action is applied automatically.

(2) Tap on the **Flag** button to add a flag to the current email

(3) Tap on the **More** button to access a range of options. Use these to **Reply**, **Reply All** or **Forward** an email. You can also **Mark** it in the same way as on page 176, or **Show Related Messages**, which are ones included in a conversation where people have replied to an original message

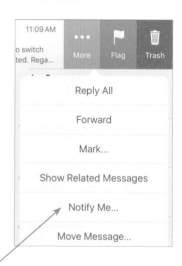

Hot tip

Some of the options from the **More** button in Step 3 are also available from this button on the top toolbar of an email.

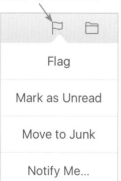

(4) Tap on the **Notify Me...** button to receive a notification when someone replies to an email in a conversation

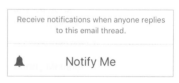

(5) For the **Mark as Read/Unread** options, tap on the **Read** or **Unread** buttons to mark emails in this way

Email Apps

The App Store contains a number of email apps that can connect to a range of email accounts. Some to look at are:

CloudMagic

This can be used to link to web-based email accounts including Gmail, Hotmail, Yahoo!, iCloud and also IMAP email accounts. Several emails can be selected at the same time in the Inbox and actions applied to them as a group. Emails can also be added as favorites by tapping on the star button. Press and hold on the email to select a time for a reminder for sending a reply.

myMail

Another option for linking one or more of your email accounts. The app also offers its own email service, called **my.com**

Messages are identified with avatars and icons so they can be found quickly, and there is a Shortcuts bar that can be accessed by swiping from right to left on an email.

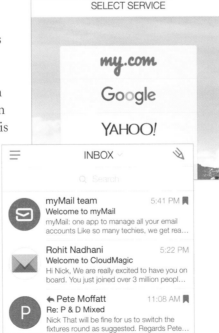

Don't forget

IMAP stands for Internet Message Access Protocol and is a method of delivering email over the internet. It is used to access emails on an email server and does not have to be a web-based service. It is a more recent protocol than POP3 (Post Office Protocol). IMAP and POP3 are more widely used in business email systems but most web-based services also support both protocols.

Beware

If you allow myMail to access your Contacts app (you will be asked this when you first log in) then photos of your contacts will be displayed next to their emails (if you have added their photos in the Contacts app).

Beware

If MailMag is set up for push notifications, i.e. it will push your emails into your Inbox at regular intervals rather than you downloading them, then your email account login details (email and password) will be stored on their server (encrypted and securely).

Hot tip

Two other email apps to look at are Hop, which can also be used to connect to people in real-time, and Cannonball Email, which has a useful feature for separating different types of emails according to their content.

...cont'd

MailMag

This has a more graphical interface to make the task of dealing with emails as appealing as possible. It can connect to the standard range of web-based and other types of email accounts.

You can select a cover for your account and there are also mailboxes, known as magazines, for storing emails with specific types of content.

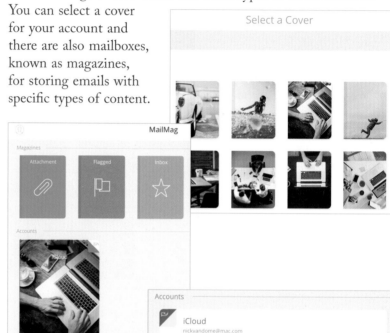

You get to your Inbox by tapping on your account cover photo, which then opens up like a magazine. Tap on an item to view it at full size and send and receive emails. Emails are organized in a grid rather than a list format, and tools for individual emails can be accessed in the magazine mailboxes by swiping down from the top of an email.

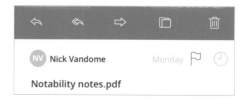

11 Printing and Scanning

This chapter shows how to print and scan documents.

AirPrint for iPad

When the iPad was first introduced, printing was one of its weaknesses. This was because there were not external ports with which to connect a printer and so printing relied on the iPad's AirPrint option for wireless printing, or third-party printing apps. Since then, AirPrint has advanced considerably and it is now possible to use a range of wireless printers to print content from your iPad.

Setting up printers

AirPrint works with wireless printers over a Local Area Network (LAN). This means that the printer and the iPad have to be connected to the same network in order to communicate with each other. This is done through a Wi-Fi router: when the printer is first turned on there will be a control panel that can be used to enter the Wi-Fi settings; usually the password for the router. Once the printer is connected to the Wi-Fi network, it should be able to communicate with your iPad.

Accessing printers

Because a lot of iPad apps do not have traditional toolbars in the same way as apps on desktop or laptop computers do, accessing Print commands is slightly different, depending on the app:

Don't forget

Printing apps can still be used to print from an iPad, but as more apps gain built-in printing functionality the necessity for them is decreasing.

Hot tip

Some wireless printers can connect directly to an iPad, without the need to connect to a network via a router.

182

1 Some apps such as Apple's iWork productivity suite, Pages, Numbers and Keynote, have a **Tools** button from which the **Print** command is accessed

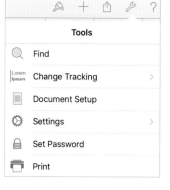

2 In other apps, such as Notes and Photos, the **Share** button can be used to access the **Print** command

Beware

The **Share** buttons in Pages, Numbers and Keynote do not have a **Print** option; this is only available from the **Tools** buttons.

Printing Documents

Once an AirPrint-enabled Wi-Fi printer has been connected and set up, it can be used to print documents from your iPad:

1 Access the **Print** function in either of the ways shown on the previous page. Tap on the **Select Printer** button

2 Available printers are listed. Tap on the **i** symbol to view information about a specific printer

3 Check the **Printer Info** to ensure it is the correct printer and tap on the **Printer** button to go back one step

4 Tap on the **Printer Options** button in Step 2 to go back to the Printer Options window. Tap on these buttons to specify the number of copies to be printed

Beware

If you are connecting to a networked printer in your workplace, check the details with your IT Administrator first.

Don't forget

The icons next to the printer name in Step 3 indicate whether it contains colored or black inks, or both.

Don't forget

The Printer Options window contains a Print Preview of the document, at the bottom of the window. Swipe left and right to view the individual pages to be printed.

...cont'd

5 Tap on the **Options** button in Step 4 and tap on the **Range** button, to specify a print page range

Range	All Pages >

6 Tap on the **All Pages** button, or drag on these barrels to set a specific page range, e.g. if you only want to print a single page of a long document. Tap on the **Printer Options** button

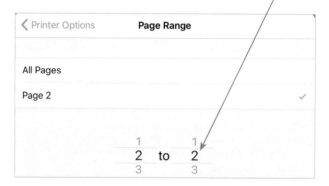

If you are printing a draft document and it contains graphics or photos, select **Black & White** in order to save the color ink in your printer. This can be used for the final version.

7 Drag the **Double-sided** and **Black & White** buttons **On** or **Off**, as required. The selected printer options are displayed here

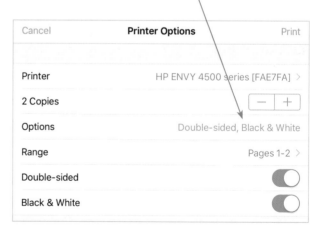

Use **Double-sided** printing for draft documents, to save paper.

Double-sided printing is also known as duplex.

8 Tap on the **Print** button to print the document with the settings specified in the Printer Options window

Print

Scanning Documents

Within the App Store there are several apps that can be used to produce high quality scanned versions of documents. These include:

- Typed or handwritten documents

- Barcodes

- Airline boarding passes

Scanning is done by taking a photo of the document, so you have to allow the app access to your iPad's camera. The document is then usually converted into a PDF file. To use a scanning app:

1 Download a scanning app such as Scanbot from the App Store

2 Tap on the app to open it. Tap on the **OK** button when the app asks if it can access your iPad's camera

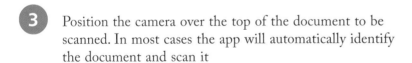

"Scanbot" Would Like to Access the Camera

In order to be able to scan documents with your device, Scanbot needs access to your camera.

| Don't Allow | OK |

3 Position the camera over the top of the document to be scanned. In most cases the app will automatically identify the document and scan it

...cont'd

Don't forget

Once a scan has been completed, tap on the **Crop** button to crop the area of the completed scanned image.

Hot tip

A Black & White filter can be effective for plain text, although it can sometimes look a bit harsh. A Gray filter can give a more even effect for text.

Don't forget

Once a scanned document has been saved it is available in the scanning app's library. From here it can be shared to an online cloud storage service, such as iCloud, or shared via email.

4 The document is scanned and displayed in the app

5 Filters can be applied to enhance the scanned document. Tap on this button to access the filters

6 Select a filter style

7 The filter style is applied to the scanned document

8 Tap on the **Save** button to save the scanned document within the scanning app

Index

R

S